Acts of Our

Gentle God

The Glorious Dawning of a New Day
on the Character of God

The Case for a Nonviolent God:
A Study to Challenge Misconceptions
About God and Offer an Encouraging
Alternative Perspective

Jay A. Schulberg

WESTBOW
P R E S S®
A DIVISION OF THOMAS NELSON
& ZONDERVAN

Scripture quotations are taken from the King James Version of the Bible.

This book is a work of non-fiction. Unless otherwise noted, the author and the publisher make no explicit guarantees as to the accuracy of the information contained in this book and in some cases, names of people and places have been altered to protect their privacy.

Content editing: Julie Schulberg
Cover design and photography: Julie Schulberg
Front cover: January Sunrise Over Lake Superior
"Unto you that fear [appreciate] my name [character] shall the Sun of righteousness [Jesus Christ] arise with healing [salvation] in his wings" (Mal. 4:2).
Back cover: The Snow Princess; the author and Gloria

WestBow Press books may be ordered through booksellers or by contacting:

WestBow Press
A Division of Thomas Nelson & Zondervan
1663 Liberty Drive
Bloomington, IN 47403
www.westbowpress.com
1 (866) 928-1240

ISBN: 978-1-5127-8083-3 (sc)
ISBN: 978-1-5127-8082-6 (hc)
ISBN: 978-1-5127-8084-0 (e)

Library of Congress Control Number: 2017904482

Print information available on the last page.

WestBow Press rev. date: 4/12/2017

Contents

Preface

Have You Ever Wondered?

In legal language, a disaster that is due entirely to the forces of nature and could not reasonably have been prevented is referred to as an *act of God*. This phrase is often included in insurance policies. Where did we get the idea God is responsible for bad things that happen in our world? Does he arbitrarily decide when and where events such as tornadoes, earthquakes, hurricanes, floods, and other natural disasters occur? Does God do something to make these things happen? Does he manipulate the natural world to bring about his desired outcome? And why doesn't he do more to prevent suffering in our world? Finally, was God responsible for the violence we read about in the Bible? Did *he* resort to violence himself?

The Bible offers answers to these questions, but we need to look beneath the surface to find them. We also need to be willing to hear what God says about himself and how he works even if it challenges beliefs we have about him.

This book will examine the character of God as revealed in the Bible—what his actions are and, just as importantly, what they are not. Many believe that God loves us when we follow his rules but is angered by our wrongdoing and punishes those who go against his dictates. The purpose of this study is to show from the Bible that God has *never* acted as a destroyer but only as a Creator, Sustainer, and Savior.

But the wisdom that is from above is first pure, then peaceable, gentle, and easy to be entreated, full of mercy and good fruits, without partiality, and without hypocrisy.

—James 3:17

1

Does It Really Matter?

Why is it important to know what God is like? Does it matter what we think about God? Does it even matter if we think about him at all? The answers to these questions lie at the very foundation of *everything* worth knowing. What we believe about God and his character determines *our* own character—and our character is more valuable than all the material riches this world has to offer.

Jesus said, "I and my Father are one" (John 10:30). God the Father and God the Son are *one* in purpose—*one* in character. Their relationship is one of perfect harmony. The writer of Hebrews declares that Jesus is to God the Father "the brightness of his glory, and the express image of his person" (Heb. 1:3). God's glory is more than just his splendor; it is his character. When Moses asked God to show him his glory, God passed by before Moses and proclaimed his character:

> The LORD, the LORD God, merciful and gracious, longsuffering, and abundant in goodness and truth, Keeping mercy for thousands, forgiving iniquity and transgression and sin. (Ex. 34:6–7)

To know God as he *really* is reconciles us to him. This knowledge is healing and life giving. Hear what Jesus said in his prayer to his Father: "And this is life eternal, that they might know thee the only true God, and Jesus Christ, whom thou hast sent" (John 17:3). Jesus demonstrated by his words and life exactly what God the Father is like. He said, "Verily, verily, I say unto you, The Son can do nothing of himself, but what he seeth the Father do: for what things soever he doeth, these also doeth the Son likewise" (John 5:19).

When we know that God is *consistently* loving and merciful, we will be drawn to him in love and trust. We are assured of God's love and good will toward us at all times, because his ways *never* change. God declares in Malachi 3:6, "For I am the LORD, I change not." He is not changeable like we are. We can be kind, loving, and thoughtful as long as we are treated fairly and with respect, but when we encounter those who cause us harm, it is our inclination to become angry and want to retaliate. God *never* responds in anger or with retaliation.

God's Word affirms that Jesus doesn't change and neither does the Father: "Jesus Christ the same yesterday, and to day, and for ever" (Heb. 13:8). "Every good gift and every perfect gift is from above, and cometh down from the Father of lights, with whom is no variableness, neither shadow of turning" (James 1:17). These words also assure us that our gentle God *does not* have a violent side.

And the Word was made flesh, and dwelt among us, (and we beheld his glory, the glory as of the only begotten of the Father,) full of grace and truth.

—John 1:14

2

Our Perfect Pattern

In the heart of the Sermon on the Mount, Jesus gives us the perfect pattern of how to live in a hostile world:

> Ye have heard that it hath been said, Thou shalt love thy neighbour, and hate thine enemy. But I say unto you, Love your enemies, bless them that curse you, do good to them that hate you, and pray for them which despitefully use you, and persecute you; That ye may be the children of your Father which is in heaven: for he maketh his sun to rise on the evil and on the good, and sendeth rain on the just and on the unjust. For if ye love them which love you, what reward have ye? do not even the publicans the same? And if ye salute your brethren only, what do ye more than others? do not even the publicans so? Be ye therefore perfect, even as your Father which is in heaven is perfect. (Matt. 5:43–48)

What does this passage teach us about God? Jesus says, "Love your enemies," and follows with, "That ye may be the children of your Father which is in heaven," and he concludes with, "Be ye therefore perfect, even as your Father which is in heaven is perfect." Jesus is asking us to treat our enemies just as our Heavenly Father treats his enemies. He wants us to understand that the elevated principles he sets before us in the Sermon on the Mount are attainable *only* as we see them originating from God himself.

In the life of Jesus, we find our perfect pattern for how to treat our enemies. Never once did he retaliate against those who wronged him. From his betrayal and arrest to his crucifixion, when he asked for his persecutors to be forgiven—"Father, forgive them; for they know not what they do" (Luke 23:34)—he demonstrated only love.

When Jesus was not welcomed at a Samaritan village, his disciples James and John thought that the village should be destroyed by fire: "Lord, wilt thou that we command fire to come down from heaven, and consume them, even as Elias did? But he turned, and rebuked them, and said, Ye know not what manner of spirit ye are of. For the Son of man is not come to destroy men's lives, but to save them" (Luke 9:54–56).

The best way for us to know what God is like is by studying the life of Jesus. He never killed anyone or threatened to do so. Jesus never hurt anyone. He never condemned anyone. When Philip, on behalf of the disciples, asked Jesus to show them the Father, he replied:

> Have I been so long time with you, and yet hast thou not known me, Philip? he that hath seen me hath seen the Father; and how sayest thou then, Shew us the Father? Believest thou not that I am in the Father, and the Father in me? the words that I speak unto you I speak not of myself: but the Father that dwelleth in me, he doeth the works. (John 14:9–10)

As we embark on a study that will challenge the theological status quo, let us determine to keep the words of Jesus and his perfect example in the forefront of our minds.

3

Our Source of Life

With some preliminary groundwork establishing the truth that God is consistently loving, we will examine God's actions in the Bible that seem to be the opposite from the principles taught by Jesus. In the book of Isaiah, we find profound insight about God's ways and thoughts:

> For my thoughts are not your thoughts, neither are your ways my ways, saith the LORD. For as the heavens are higher than the earth, so are my ways higher than your ways, and my thoughts than your thoughts. (Isa. 55:8–9)

God's ways and thoughts are infinitely higher in purpose and character than our ways and thoughts. This definitive truth about God is difficult for us to grasp. In our determination to justify ourselves, we imagine that God is like us. We get angry, so we think God must get angry like we do. We are moved to retaliate when we are wronged, so we think God must have the same disposition to retaliate when he is wronged. God tells us otherwise:

> These things hast thou done, and I kept silence; thou thoughtest that I was altogether such an one as thyself: but I will reprove thee, and set them in order before thine eyes. (Ps. 50:21)

When God created our world, he didn't intend for it to function on its own. God being uninvolved with our world would not only be contrary to his purpose, it would mean that life could not continue on our planet—"For in him we live, and move, and have our being" (Acts 17:28). God sustains us in every breath we take.

God is the Source and Sustainer of all life. However, there *is* one thing that can separate us from him—sin. But what is sin? We often think of sin as the bad things we do or breaking God's commandments. The thought is that sin can somehow be quantified, with some of us having a large quantity of it and others having not as much or even very little. In the Bible, we learn that the bad things we do are the symptoms of a deeply embedded malady we have all inherited from our first parents. This malady is believing the lie that God is looking out for his own best interests. This lie of the devil was bequeathed to the human race in the garden of Eden, and it has distorted our picture of God ever since.

When God created Adam and Eve and placed them in the garden, they were given one restriction—and only one:

> And the LORD God commanded the man, saying, Of every tree of the garden thou mayest freely eat: But of the tree of the knowledge of good and evil, thou shalt not eat of it: for in the day that thou eatest thereof thou shalt surely die. (Gen. 2:16–17)

It is easy to understand why God placed the "tree of life" (Gen. 2:9) in the garden, but it is difficult for us to appreciate *why* he placed "the tree of the knowledge of good and evil" in that perfect environment. At first thought, we might see the presence of that tree, with the warning against eating from it, as an invitation to disaster.

4

Made in His Image

In Genesis we find our heritage: "And God said, Let us make man in our image, after our likeness: ... So God created man in his own image, in the image of God created he him; male and female created he them" (Gen. 1:26–27). What does it mean to be made in God's image, and what *is* God's image? We will discover what God's image is when we find a definition that describes who God is. The precise definition is found in 1 John 4:8: "God is love." Notice that the verse does not only say "God is loving," as if *love* is one of his many characteristics, but it says simply, "God *is* love." Anything else that we can know about God must be in harmony with this definition. Therefore, just as God is perfect, we can reasonably conclude that the love of God must be perfect also, without a shred of self-interest. Furthermore, his love must be *unchangeable* as he is unchangeable.

If we are made in the image of God, then we must be created by God to *experience* love. Now love, to *be* love, cannot be dictated or in any way compelled. It can only be freely given as a choice. This is easily understood if we imagine a love-starved person with a loaded gun boarding a bus and demanding love from the passengers on threat of death. Would this method generate love?

Suppose we were to try a less drastic way of obtaining love by building a robot that was programed to say "I love you" when we come into its presence. Would this result in a satisfying and meaningful love-based relationship? Could these methods, which would fail to secure love for us, work for God?

Let's go back to the garden of Eden and that perplexing forbidden tree. If God had not made that tree, would it have been possible for humankind to love as God loves? For love, to be love, requires that it be freely given. For love to be freely given, we must also have the liberty to not love. Love is always a choice; love cannot be commanded or coerced.

If God would have created our first parents and placed them in the garden without providing some tangible way whereby they could have chosen not to love and trust him, it would not have been possible for them to love as God himself loves. Just as God is our Source of life, he is also our Source of genuine love—life and love are inseparable. To be created in God's image gives each of us the potential to become a loving friend to our Creator.

God did not place the tree of the knowledge of good and evil with the restriction forbidding eating from its branches as an arbitrary test of our obedience to him, but as an assurance that he values our freedom of choice so highly that he was willing to take the risk that we could choose to turn from him. When we understand the reason why God placed the forbidden tree in the garden, we will not accuse him of being a self-serving dictator. There was one, however, who was ready to accuse God of that very thing.

5

The Master Deceiver

Now the serpent was more subtil than any beast of the field which the LORD God had made. And he said unto the woman, Yea, hath God said, Ye shall not eat of every tree of the garden? And the woman said unto the serpent, We may eat of the fruit of the trees of the garden: But the fruit of the tree which is in the midst of the garden, God hath said, Ye shall not eat of it, neither shall ye touch it, lest ye die. And *the serpent said* unto the woman, *Ye shall not surely die: For God doth know that in the day ye eat thereof, then your eyes shall be opened, and ye shall be as gods, knowing good and evil.*
—Genesis 3:1–5, (emphasis added)

First, let's determine the identity of this talking snake. Who is this serpent? "And the great dragon was cast out, that old serpent, called the Devil, and Satan, which deceiveth the whole world: he was cast out into the earth, and his angels were cast out with him" (Rev. 12:9). Eve was not just talking with an intelligent snake, but with Satan—the master deceiver himself.

The serpent by subtle insinuation accused God of lying to Adam and Eve and withholding something good from them. Furthermore, if they were to simply eat the fruit, their eyes would be opened, and they would become like "gods, knowing good and evil." Who did the woman chose to believe, God or Satan?

> And when the woman saw that the tree was good for food, and that it was pleasant to the eyes, and a tree to be desired to make one wise, she took of the fruit thereof, and did eat, and gave also unto her husband with her; and he did eat. And the eyes of them both were opened, and they knew that they were naked; and they sewed fig leaves together, and made themselves aprons. And they heard the voice of the LORD God walking in the garden in the cool of the day: and Adam and his wife hid themselves from the presence of the LORD God amongst the trees of the garden. And the LORD God called unto Adam, and said unto him, Where art thou? (Gen. 3:6–9)

When Adam and Eve ate from the forbidden tree, their eyes were opened (they became self-conscious), and they sought to hide themselves from God. What was God's response? He came looking for them. His first words were, "Where art thou?" He sought the reconciliation of his now estranged children.

> For the Son of man is come to seek and to save that which was lost.
>
> —Jesus (Luke 19:10)

6

What Is Sin?

Now, getting back to the question: what is sin? To find the correct definition, it is important that we first identify exactly what went wrong at the "tree of the knowledge of good and evil." In Genesis 3:6, the woman saw three desirable qualities of the tree:

1. "The tree was good for food." On the surface this may appear to be true, were it not for the fact that the tree was forbidden as a source of food. The problem was not with the fruit itself but that the woman was now looking at it as *good*.

2. The tree was "pleasant to the eyes." Everything that God created in the garden was perfect, therefore the tree would in fact be "pleasant to the eyes." The woman saw one more *desirable* quality of the tree.

3. "A tree desired to make one wise." Really? Did this tree have mystical qualities? Was the serpent right? Would having a knowledge of good and evil *really* be desirable? And what does having a knowledge of good and evil mean? Is it just acquiring information?

The verse concludes with "she took of the fruit thereof, and did eat, and gave also unto her husband with her; and he did eat." This is often understood to be humanity's first sin, but *what* is the sin? What came first—eating the fruit or believing the serpent's lie about God?

The primary problem was when Eve believed the serpent's lie that God was selfishly withholding something good from them. Sin is not just the action itself, as if sin is a quantifiable substance. Sin, at its core, is a pathological condition of the mind that sees God as one who is self-centered and thus being unable to trust him.

Sin can be compared to a disease. In a disease there is an underlying cause such as a bacterial infection, a metabolic disorder, or an immune system dysfunction. These primary causes result in one or more symptoms: fever, nausea, pain, dizziness, lethargy, and so on. With sin, the primary cause is believing the lie about God and, as a result, alienating ourselves from him whose love is other-centered. Our outward *sins* (the symptoms) are the result of believing that God is self-serving (the pathological cause). Jesus, in his conversation with the scribes and Pharisees, used this analogy of sin being a disease in need of healing:

> And when the scribes and Pharisees saw him eat with publicans and sinners, they said unto his disciples, How is it that he eateth and drinketh with publicans and sinners? When Jesus heard it, he saith unto them, They that are whole have no need of the physician, but *they that are sick*: I came not to call the righteous, but *sinners* to repentance. (Mark 2:16–17, emphasis added)

Sin is deadly because it separates us from God, the Source of all life. In this separation that occurs, it is never God separating himself from us—it is always us separating ourselves from him. Adam and Eve became afraid of God rather than Satan—the one they *should* have feared. After eating the fruit, the Bible says, "Adam and his wife hid themselves from the presence of the LORD God amongst the trees of the garden" (Gen. 3:8). We have been hiding from our gentle God since that day.

We would do well to note that when God warned Adam and Eve not to eat from the forbidden tree, he did *not* say, "On the day that you eat of it, I will kill you." He said, "In the day that thou eatest thereof thou shalt surely die." When the man and his wife ate of the tree, the process of dying began in them on that very day as they separated themselves from their Life Source. It is sin (believing the lie that God is selfish and untrustworthy) that is deadly, not God: "For the wages of sin is death" (Rom. 6:23). God is not in the sin business, and he doesn't pay the wages of sin.

It is also apparent that when Adam and Eve ate the fruit of the forbidden tree, they received much more than head knowledge of good and evil. They unwittingly committed themselves and their descendants to *experience* the knowledge of good and evil. They would not merely know *about* evil; they would think it, they would live it, they would be enslaved to it, and as a result they would *know* pain, suffering, fear, and death.

Humankind was not alone in suffering the inevitable consequences when sin entered our world. All nature was affected by the disharmony between creation and Creator that was initiated by Adam and Eve's sin: "For we know that the whole creation groaneth and travaileth in pain together until now" (Rom. 8:22). The earth became a dangerous place for humankind and the animals. Since the flood of Noah's day, the earth has been subject to violent weather, earthquakes, volcanos, and other catastrophic forces of nature. The violent forces evident in nature are not from God; they exist only because *we* have put God at a distance from us.

7

Why Is There a Devil?

Reference has already been made to a literal spiritual being set in opposition to God. This being is referred to in the Bible as Satan, the devil, the serpent, leviathan, and Lucifer as well as several other titles.

Compared to two hundred years ago, a much smaller percentage of people in Western civilization today believe in a literal devil. In our modern culture, Satan is often relegated to the realm of superstition and ignorance. It is with this thought in mind, and in answer to the question, that we will examine the biblical account of Satan (the adversary).

Satan is identified in the Bible as a fallen angel. The term *fallen* implies that Satan was originally a sinless being who chose to rebel against his Creator. Why he rebelled against God is a mystery, considering the perfect environment of heaven. Apparently, he held a position of honor and influence among the angels. At some point in time, a seed of pride germinated and grew resulting in dissatisfaction with his position in heaven. This eventually culminated in open revolt against God.

Satan was not alone in his rebellion. He was able to gain support from many of the other angels, although the majority of the angels chose to remain loyal to God. The war that resulted from the rebellion of Satan and his followers was not a war involving physical weapons such as those used in this world's conflicts. God prevailed in this heavenly war by using

14

love against selfishness, truth against deception, transparency against secrecy, reason against irrationality, patience against desperation, and trust against suspicion.

It is reasonable to believe that the methods used by Satan on Eve in the garden of Eden to cause her alienation from God were the very same ones practiced earlier by him to gain followers to his cause in heaven. Until that time, a question about God's fairness had never been brought before the heavenly angels. They had no way of knowing with absolute certainty whether Satan's charges against God had any validity, or not. For this reason Satan has been given the opportunity to demonstrate his way of governing.

We might question why God didn't destroy his antagonist at the beginning of the rebellion. Wouldn't that have prevented the escalation of the rebellion? No, that would have only confirmed to the angels that Satan's charges against God *did* have validity. Had God destroyed Satan, the very act would have negated freedom making it an empty ideal with no substance. There is something else besides this. To be consistent in our study of the Bible, the weight of evidence demonstrates that God never destroys—sin does. Satan *will* eventually be destroyed. This destruction will not come from God, but from Satan's own sin:

> Moreover the word of the LORD came unto me, saying, Son of man, take up a lamentation upon the king of Tyrus, and say unto him, Thus saith the Lord GOD; Thou sealest up the sum, full of wisdom, and perfect in beauty. Thou hast been in Eden the garden of God; every precious stone was thy covering, the sardius, topaz, and the diamond, the beryl, the onyx,

and the jasper, the sapphire, the emerald, and the carbuncle, and gold: the workmanship of thy tabrets and of thy pipes was prepared in thee in the day that thou wast created. *Thou art the anointed cherub that covereth; and I have set thee so: thou wast upon the holy mountain of God; thou hast walked up and down in the midst of the stones of fire. Thou wast perfect in thy ways from the day that thou wast created, till iniquity was found in thee.* By the multitude of thy merchandise they have filled the midst of thee with violence, and thou hast sinned: therefore I will cast thee as profane out of the mountain of God: and I will destroy thee, O covering cherub, from the midst of the stones of fire. *Thine heart was lifted up because of thy beauty, thou hast corrupted thy wisdom by reason of thy brightness:* I will cast thee to the ground, I will lay thee before kings, that they may behold thee. Thou hast defiled thy sanctuaries by the multitude of thine iniquities, by the iniquity of thy traffick; *therefore will I bring forth a fire from the midst of thee, it shall devour thee*, and I will bring thee to ashes upon the earth in the sight of all them that behold thee. All they that know thee among the people shall be astonished at thee: thou shalt be a terror, and *never shalt thou be any more.* (Ezek. 28:11–19, emphasis added)

The king of Tyrus fittingly typifies Satan in this account. Satan was created perfect, without a trace of pride or selfishness. His fall from perfection was his own doing, and he had no excuse for the course he took. He became proud because of his beauty. The "fire" that will destroy Satan will not come from an outside source; it will come from within Satan himself. This fire is his own selfishness. It is this self-generated fire that will devour him. Satan will cease to exist—"never shalt thou be anymore."

> How art thou fallen from heaven, O Lucifer, son of the morning! how art thou cut down to the ground, which didst weaken the nations! For thou hast said in thine heart, *I will ascend* into heaven, *I will exalt* my throne above the stars of God: *I will sit* also upon the mount of the congregation, in the sides of the north: *I will ascend* above the heights of the clouds; *I will be like the most High.* (Isa. 14:12–14, emphasis added)

Lucifer (Satan's original title) fell because he sought to exalt himself. Jesus taught his followers, "And whosoever shall exalt himself shall be abased; and he that shall humble himself shall be exalted" (Matt. 23:12). Lucifer brought about his own abasement. His words "I will be like the most High" betray the truth that he only coveted God's position. He had no interest in reflecting God's character (the only way that a created being can be *like* God).

When examining this passage, it should also be noted that the thoughts expressed about God are Lucifer's and are not an accurate description of God's motives. Lucifer, because of his obsession for self-exaltation, came to imagine that God possessed this same selfish motive.

And there was war in heaven: Michael and his angels fought against the dragon; and the dragon fought and his angels, And prevailed not; neither was their place found any more in heaven. And the great dragon was cast out, that old serpent, called the Devil, and Satan, which deceiveth the whole world: he was cast out into the earth, and his angels were cast out with him. (Rev. 12:7–9)

This passage documents the war in heaven where Satan began his work of deception. His work has not been confined to a little corner of our planet; he has deceived "the whole world."

And he said unto them, I beheld Satan as lightning fall from heaven. (Luke 10:18)

Jesus speaks here of the rapidity of Satan's fall from loyalty to insurrection.

For we are made a spectacle unto the world, and to angels, and to men. (1 Cor. 4:9)

By them that have preached the gospel unto you with the Holy Ghost sent down from heaven; which things the angels desire to look into. (1 Peter 1:12)

When Satan rebelled in heaven, taking with him a number of the angels, the remaining loyal angels did not fully understand what was happening and why. The gospel message is for them, as well as it is for us, and they are intensely interested in God's selfless efforts on this earth to save humankind from self-destruction. The "everlasting gospel" (Rev. 14:6) is the assurance that the universe will be eternally secure from any doubt about God's trustworthiness: "What do ye imagine against the LORD? he will make an utter end: affliction shall not rise up the second time" (Nah. 1:9).

Then was Jesus led up of the Spirit into the wilderness to be tempted of the devil. And when he had fasted forty days and forty nights, he was afterward an hungred. And when the tempter came to him, he said, *If thou be the Son of God*, command that these stones be made bread. But he answered and said, It is written, Man shall not live by bread alone, but by every word that proceedeth out of the mouth of God. Then the devil taketh him up into the holy city, and setteth him on a pinnacle of the temple, And saith unto him, *If thou be the Son of God*, cast thyself down: for it is written, He shall give his angels charge concerning thee: and in their hands they shall bear thee up, lest at any time thou dash thy foot against a stone. Jesus said unto him, It is written again, Thou shalt not tempt the Lord thy God. Again, the devil taketh him up into an exceeding high mountain, and sheweth him all the kingdoms of the world, and the glory of them; And saith unto him, All these things will I give thee, if thou wilt fall down and worship me. Then saith Jesus unto him, Get thee hence, Satan: for it is written, Thou shalt worship the Lord thy God, and him only shalt

thou serve. Then the devil leaveth him, and,
behold, angels came and ministered unto him.
(Matt. 4:1–11, emphasis added)

Satan came to Jesus as a tempter; his apparent objective being to sever Jesus's trust in and dependence on his Father. Satan achieved success using a similar approach on Eve in the garden of Eden. Satan was determined to thwart Jesus's purpose of coming to this world to save humankind by tempting Jesus to use his divine power to benefit himself. The deceiver was desperate to prevent Jesus from succeeding in his mission of revealing God's *unselfishness*—which would expose Satan for the liar that he is.

In one temptation the devil offered Jesus the "kingdoms of the world" if Jesus would only fall down and worship him. It is noteworthy that Jesus did not contest the devil's claim to jurisdiction over the "kingdoms of the world." When God first created humans, he gave humankind dominion "over all the earth" (Gen. 1:26), but when Adam and Eve believed Satan's lie about their Creator, they essentially handed over this dominion to the devil. We see deception, oppression, coercion, and inequality in the "kingdoms of the world." In God's kingdom no force is used at any time or under any circumstance. There is no similarity between his kingdom and the kingdoms of this world, which rely on the rule of law rather than the law of love.

Hereafter I will not talk much with you: for the
prince of this world cometh, and hath nothing
in me. (John 14:30)

Jesus affirms that it is Satan who is "the prince of this world." When we deny the existence of Satan and his widespread influence on our planet, we unwittingly lay the blame on God for our suffering.

> Be sober, be vigilant; because your adversary the devil, as a roaring lion, walketh about, seeking whom he may devour. (1 Peter 5:8)

The devil is our adversary—*not* God.

> Put on the whole armour of God, that ye may be able to stand against the wiles of the devil. For we wrestle not against flesh and blood, but against principalities, against powers, against the rulers of the darkness of this world, against spiritual wickedness in high places. (Eph. 6:11–12)

When we realize we are all victims of the deception about God foisted on the human race, we will not look at other people as our enemies, but as fellow victims of this massive deception.

> And they had a king over them, which is the angel of the bottomless pit, whose name in the Hebrew tongue is Abaddon, but in the Greek tongue hath his name Apollyon. (Rev. 9:11)

The "angel of the bottomless pit" refers to Satan. Apollyon, the name given him here, means *destroyer* in the Greek. *Satan* is the destroyer. Would we have any justification for effectively giving our gentle God this same title?

8

The Destroying Serpent

The plagues that God sent against the Egyptians seem to be some of God's most deliberate acts of destruction. On the surface there appears to be no other way to interpret these events in the Bible. Recall, though, the verse we read earlier: "For my thoughts are not your thoughts, neither are your ways my ways, saith the LORD" (Isa. 55:8).

Moses was commissioned by God to lead the children of Israel from Egyptian bondage to freedom. He was to go before Pharaoh to warn him of the disasters that were about to take place in his country. When God met Moses in the wilderness, he gave him an object lesson that Moses and Aaron would later demonstrate before Pharaoh that would show the ruler exactly what God's role would be in the coming catastrophic events:

> And the LORD said unto him, What is that in thine hand? And he said, A rod. And he said, Cast it on the ground. And he cast it on the ground, and it became a serpent; and Moses fled from before it. And the LORD said unto Moses, Put forth thine hand, and take it by the tail. And he put forth his hand, and caught it, and it became a rod in his hand. (Ex. 4:2–4)

> And he said, Is not Aaron the Levite thy brother? I know that he can speak well. ... And

he shall be thy spokesman unto the people:
and he shall be, even he shall be to thee instead
of a mouth, and thou shalt be to him instead
of God. And thou shalt take this rod in thine
hand, wherewith thou shalt do signs. (Ex. 4:14,
16–17)

Moses was to go before Pharaoh as God's representative.
God's purpose in this demonstration was for it to be more
than a mere display of power; it was an illustration to identify
the *real* destroyer. When Moses, as God's representative, held
the rod in his hand, it symbolized the forces of nature under
God's control. No harm could come to Egypt as long as God's
protective hand held back the destructive forces of nature.
When Moses cast down the rod, it became a serpent, the
symbol of evil and destruction. This symbolized the forces of
nature out of God's control and under the control of Satan—
the destroyer.

Hundreds of years before the time of Moses and after
Joseph (who had been sold into slavery by his half-brothers)
had interpreted Pharaoh's disturbing dreams, there was
a much better arrangement for the children of Israel.
Pharaoh elevated Joseph to a place of honor and respect for
interpreting the prophetic dreams and for his foresight in
preparing the nation for a seven-year famine. Joseph's family
had been warmly welcomed. The Egyptians demonstrated
their appreciation for Joseph and the God he worshipped.
God was able to richly bless the nation. Many years after the
death of Joseph, however, the Egyptians forgot about him
and his God and made slaves of the children of Israel who had
prospered and multiplied in the land. The Egyptians, by their
actions, were sending the message that they did not desire

God's presence. They had their own gods and did not want to acknowledge the God of their slaves. God was no longer able to continue his full measure of blessing and protection while at the same time allowing the Egyptians their freedom to separate from him.

If at any time after the plagues had begun, Pharaoh would have turned from his defiant course and let the Israelites go, God would have taken control of the forces of nature again, and the plagues would have ended. The stubborn ruler did not do this, and Egypt was left in ruin. God's role in the plagues of Egypt becomes clear when we consider the symbolic message that God gave in the rod and the serpent.

Additional support to exonerate God from charges of destruction by natural elements is found in the book of 1 Kings. The prophet Elijah at a low point in his ministry was hiding in a cave from Queen Jezebel, who had threatened his life. God came to his runaway prophet:

> And he said unto him, What doest thou here, Elijah? And he said, I have been very jealous for the LORD God of hosts: for the children of Israel have forsaken thy covenant, thrown down thine altars, and slain thy prophets with the sword; and I, even I only, am left; and they seek my life, to take it away. And he said, Go forth, and stand upon the mount before the LORD. *And, behold, the LORD passed by*, and a great and strong wind rent the mountains, and brake in pieces the rocks before the LORD; but the LORD *was not* in the wind: and after the wind an earthquake; but the LORD *was not* in the earthquake: And after the earthquake a

fire; but the LORD *was not* in the fire: and after the fire *a still small voice.* (1 Kings 19:9–12, emphasis added)

Our gentle God still speaks most audibly in a still small voice.

The thief cometh not, but for to steal, and to kill, and to destroy: I am come that they might have life, and that they might have it more abundantly.

—Jesus (John 10:10)

9

The Captivity of Job

The book of Job provides clear evidence of Satan's role in acts of suffering and destruction. It also gives us a glimpse behind the scenes into the spiritual battle between God and the forces of evil. Job, "a perfect and an upright man" (Job 1:8), found himself caught in intense crossfire at a critical juncture in this spiritual battle:

> Now there was a day when the sons of God came to present themselves before the LORD, and Satan came also among them. And the LORD said unto Satan, Whence comest thou? Then Satan answered the LORD, and said, From going to and fro in the earth, and from walking up and down in it. And the LORD said unto Satan, Hast thou considered my servant Job, that there is none like him in the earth, a perfect and an upright man, one that feareth God, and escheweth evil? Then Satan answered the LORD, and said, Doth Job fear God for nought? Hast not thou made an hedge about him, and about his house, and about all that he hath on every side? thou hast blessed the work of his hands, and his substance is increased in the land. But put forth thine hand now, and touch all that he hath, and he will curse thee to thy face. And the LORD said unto

Satan, Behold, all that he hath is in thy power; only upon himself put not forth thine hand. So Satan went forth from the presence of the LORD. (Job 1:6–12)

Satan immediately set out to destroy everything Job had, including his sons and daughters. In the destruction that followed, Satan resorted to the use of enemy raiders "the Sabeans" (v. 15) and "the Chaldeans" (v. 17), "the fire of God ... from heaven" (v. 16), and "a great wind from the wilderness" (v. 19).

While it is evident in the book of Job who the destroyer is, many readers are still troubled by Job's sufferings because it is erroneously assumed that God *let* Satan afflict Job. The thought is since God is all-powerful, he should have prevented Satan's attack on Job. However, God's power was never the relevant issue at stake; it has always been and always will be about God's principles of governance—is God consistent in giving his intelligent created beings freedom or is he not? Freedom, to *be* freedom, must be irrevocable; meaning that it is unalterable and cannot be recalled—regardless of circumstances.

In the case of Job, there was, in addition, something else at stake besides God's reputation—our planet. Satan was strategizing to seize our world (enemy occupied territory) as his own sovereign kingdom: "And the LORD said unto Satan, Whence comest thou? Then Satan answered the LORD, and said, From going to and fro in the earth, and from walking up and down in it" (Job 1:7).

If we take the liberty to thoughtfully read between the lines, Satan was essentially saying to God, "I have been roaming the whole earth and it appears that I have unanimous support for my cause; I claim my right to absolute rule on the earth." Throughout the drama that follows, God (thankfully) stayed one step ahead of Satan—God knew his trusting servant. Job remained faithful to God despite suffering the second most vicious satanic attack recorded in the Bible. In the end, God preserved Job's life, and "turned the captivity of Job, when he prayed for his friends" (Job 42:10), who were actually in a more perilous position than Job himself—they didn't *know* God.

The book of Job gives us insight into the spiritual battle that continues today between God and the forces of darkness. When we are able to visualize something of the incomprehensibly complex interaction of multiple free wills that God sees clearly, we will begin to appreciate the magnitude of the challenge that faces him.

We as intelligent beings are not alone in our world. There are numerous spiritual beings sharing our space with us—Satan and his army of fallen angels. Given our individual selfish natures and those of the demonic entities, our earth is the stage for multiple collisions of self-centered free wills on a daily basis. What is especially difficult for us to comprehend is how Satan and his demonic army can hinder or withstand God.

It can be unsettling for us when we realize that God does not wield absolute control and authority over everything on our planet. However, God has no desire to control our individual lives, nor is it in his nature to do so; he created us to be free intelligent beings—not puppets.

In the beginning of the book of Job, three central participants are brought to view: God, Satan, and Job. At the end of the book Satan is not mentioned by name. Why would he be absent at the critical conclusion of this monumental encounter with God?

The entire forty-first chapter of Job focuses on a mysterious creature God referred to as "leviathan." What or who is leviathan? Does the Bible provide any clues to help us identify this creature? "In that day the LORD with his sore and great and strong sword shall punish leviathan the piercing serpent, even leviathan that crooked serpent; and he shall slay the dragon that is in the sea" (Isa. 27:1). Who does "the piercing serpent," "that crooked serpent," and "the dragon that is in the sea" refer to? "And the great dragon was cast out, that old serpent, called the Devil, and Satan, which deceiveth the whole world: he was cast out into the earth, and his angels were cast out with him" (Rev. 12:9). Let's examine Job chapter forty-one with an eye to see satanic attributes in the description of this creature:

> Canst thou draw out *leviathan* with an hook? or his tongue with a cord which thou lettest down? Canst thou put an hook into his nose? or bore his jaw through with a thorn? *Will he make many supplications unto thee? will he speak soft words unto thee? Will he make a covenant with thee? wilt thou take him for a servant for ever? Wilt thou play with him as with a bird? or wilt thou bind him for thy maidens?* Shall the companions make a banquet of him? shall they part him among the merchants? Canst thou fill his skin with barbed irons? or his head with fish spears? *Lay thine hand upon him, remember the battle, do no more. Behold, the hope of him is in vain: shall not one be cast down even at the sight of him? None is so fierce that dare stir him up: who then is able to stand before me?* Who

hath prevented me, that I should repay him? whatsoever is under the whole heaven is mine. I will not conceal his parts, nor his power, nor his comely proportion. *Who can discover the face of his garment? or who can come to him with his double bridle? Who can open the doors of his face? his teeth are terrible round about. His scales are his pride, shut up together as with a close seal. One is so near to another, that no air can come between them.* They are joined one to another, they stick together, that they cannot be sundered. By his neesings a light doth shine, and his eyes are like the eyelids of the morning. *Out of his mouth go burning lamps, and sparks of fire leap out. Out of his nostrils goeth smoke, as out of a seething pot or caldron. His breath kindleth coals, and a flame goeth out of his mouth. In his neck remaineth strength, and sorrow is turned into joy before him.* The flakes of his flesh are joined together: they are firm in themselves; they cannot be moved. *His heart is as firm as a stone; yea, as hard as a piece of the nether millstone. When he raiseth up himself, the mighty are afraid: by reason of breakings they purify themselves. The sword of him that layeth at him cannot hold: the spear, the dart, nor the habergeon. He esteemeth iron as straw, and brass as rotten wood. The arrow cannot make him flee: slingstones are turned with him into stubble. Darts are counted as stubble: he laugheth at the shaking of a spear.* Sharp stones are under him: he spreadeth sharp pointed things upon the mire. *He maketh the deep to boil like a pot: he maketh the sea like a pot of ointment. He maketh a path to shine after him; one would think the deep to be hoary. Upon earth there is not his like, who is made without fear. He beholdeth all high things: he is a king over all the children of pride.* (Job 41, emphasis added)

God uses symbolic language in this chapter to describe an enemy so powerful and devoid of sympathy that we are powerless to battle this antagonist on our own. God is engaged in an intense conflict with the most formidable enemy imaginable, yet God is absolutely committed to fight this battle on our behalf without resorting to the use of force at any time or under any circumstances.

Satan has made God to appear as he is himself: angry, vindictive, unforgiving, forceful, legalistic, judgmental, and exacting, while at the same time, he appears to us as "an angel of light" (2 Cor. 11:14), but God sees clearly what we cannot see—how skilled the deceiver is at his craft.

With this symbolic description of God's antagonist, we can gain some understanding of the daily battle God wages for each of us. God *does* intervene to remove his children from harm's way when Satan oversteps his bounds in his desperation to hinder or destroy those who are responsive to the Holy Spirit. Some of these interventions are apparent to us, while most are not. Consequently, God will continue to have blame heaped on him daily for the suffering we see in our world. Hopefully the experience of Job will help us to realize that God *can't* prevent every accident, every calamity, every sickness, or every death while at the same time honoring the free wills of his intelligent creatures.

There is something else that God sees clearly. Only he is self-existent—*Satan is not*. Satan is a created being who chose evil, and evil is absolutely dependent on good for its existence. *When* all intelligent beings in the universe understand this truth, in the context of the revelation about God's trustworthiness, he will allow Satan, the originator of evil, to self-destruct; what could be fairer than that?

Fear thou not; for 1 am with thee: be not dismayed; for 1 am thy God: 1 will strengthen thee; yea, 1 will help thee; yea, 1 will uphold thee with the right hand of my righteousness.

—Isaiah 41:10

10

Why We Misread the Bible

The Bible was not written as dictation from God, "but holy men of God spake as they were moved by the Holy Ghost" (2 Peter 1:21). The Bible was written by men using their own words and within the context of the culture, background, and personality of each individual writer.

Why does it often appear in the Bible that God *is* a destroyer? To answer this question it will be helpful to first consider the religious culture of the ancient Bible lands. One thing is apparent—the Israelite people, the main characters of the Bible narrative, were surrounded by the influence of idolatry. Despite plain warnings to shun idolatry, they were continually influenced by the idolatrous practices of their neighbors. The Israelites' understanding of God had been perverted by the prevailing culture.

God longed to reveal himself to the people. However, to fully reveal the glory of his character to them would have driven them further from him. God condescended to the level of the people he wanted to reach, and he needed to speak their language to do so. He was willing to be misunderstood in his interaction with the Israelite people in order to save them from destroying themselves.

Furthermore, in the ancient Bible lands, the people under demonic influence created gods that were violent and easily angered. They believed that the calamities they suffered were caused by these angry gods. Consequently, the people brought them sacrifices to appease their anger and bowed down to them in their religious ceremonies.

In the Old Testament, relatively little mention is made of Satan, the being who is *really* to blame for the suffering and death in our world. If Satan would have been identified as the one responsible for the calamities the people suffered, their attention would have been focused on him rather than God. The Israelites would have considered Satan as another god who had impressive power over the forces of nature. This would have led them to offer sacrifices to him, and in so doing they would have worshipped Satan instead of God.

God sought to prevent this from happening by allowing himself to be seen as the source of not only the good things the people received but the *bad* things as well. God was more concerned about the people and the affect that a premature unveiling of the real destroyer's identity would have on them than he was about his own reputation. Even with this selfless condescension on God's part, the people still gave homage to demonic entities through idolatrous worship: "They sacrificed unto devils, not to God" (Deut. 32:17).

The ancient Israelites were not ready for a clear revelation of God's gentle and loving character. They would have rejected God altogether had he come to them appearing as he really is—unselfish love. They wanted a god that would fight for them and use violence against their enemies. The Israelites wanted a god that *was like themselves*. Instead of accepting the truth that "God created man in his own image" (Gen. 1:27), they were determined to *create God in their own image*. This gives us (if we are willing to consider it) understanding of how humankind has primarily related to God down through the ages to our present day.

11

Why We Misunderstand God

When God walked among us, he was not recognized or welcomed by the religious establishment:

> As they went out, behold, they brought to him a dumb man possessed with a devil. And when the devil was cast out, the dumb spake: and the multitudes marvelled, saying, It was never so seen in Israel. *But the Pharisees said, He casteth out devils through the prince of the devils.* And Jesus went about all the cities and villages, teaching in their synagogues, and preaching the gospel of the kingdom, and healing every sickness and every disease among the people. (Matt. 9:32–35, emphasis added)

The following words of Isaiah aptly apply to those who accused Jesus of being in league with Satan: "Woe unto them that call evil good, and good evil; that put darkness for light, and light for darkness; that put bitter for sweet, and sweet for bitter! Woe unto them that are wise in their own eyes" (Isa. 5:20–21).

> He was in the world, and the world was made by him, and the world knew him not. He came unto his own, and his own received him not. (John 1:10–11)

This passage is not just referring to ancient history. God continues to be unrecognized, misunderstood, and unknown. We misunderstand God because of our propensity to erroneously assume that he is self-centered like we are:

> But the natural man receiveth not the things of the Spirit of God: for they are foolishness unto him: neither can he know them, because they are spiritually discerned. (1 Cor. 2:14)

The human race has an attraction to external religion. Instead what we need is to exchange our selfishness for God's love. The thought of relinquishing selfishness is very threatening to the "natural man." External religion *seems* much safer, but this kind of safety is an insidious illusion; external religion is often used to hide from God.

> The Pharisees also came unto him [Jesus], tempting him, and saying unto him, Is it lawful for a man to put away his wife for every cause? And he answered and said unto them, Have ye not read, that he which made them at the beginning made them male and female, And said, For this cause shall a man leave father and mother, and shall cleave to his wife: and they twain shall be one flesh? Wherefore they are no more twain, but one flesh. What therefore God hath joined together, let not man put asunder. They say unto him, Why did Moses then command to give a writing of divorcement, and to put her away? He saith unto them, Moses because of the hardness of your hearts

suffered you to put away your wives: but from
the beginning it was not so. (Matt. 19:3–8)

Much of the Old Testament reflects God's efforts to come close to hardhearted people. God is misunderstood in the passages of scripture where he accommodated the will of the people rather than abandon them as hopeless. We are the ones who lack compassion—*not God*. Yet we invariably misread God's interaction with merciless people in the Old Testament. As a result, we accuse God of condoning slavery and polygamy, encouraging wars of conquest, commanding genocide, and decreeing severe penalties for lawbreakers. We make these accusations because we don't understand the magnitude of the problem related to human hardheartedness that God was continually faced with in his interaction with ancient Israel.

Jesus, in the Sermon on the Mount, magnified the law, giving it a practical application based on the law of love:

Ye have heard that it hath been said, An eye for
an eye, and a tooth for a tooth: But I say unto
you, That ye resist not evil: but whosoever shall
smite thee on thy right cheek, turn to him the
other also. And if any man will sue thee at the
law, and take away thy coat, let him have thy
cloak also. And whosoever shall compel thee to
go a mile, go with him twain. Give to him that
asketh thee, and from him that would borrow
of thee turn not thou away. (Matt. 5:38–42)

In these words, Jesus expounded on God's perfect will as opposed to his adaptation to the will of hardhearted people.

Jesus said unto them, If God were your Father, ye would love me: for I proceeded forth and came from God; neither came I of myself, but he sent me. Why do ye not understand my speech? even because ye cannot hear my word. *Ye are of your father the devil,* and the lusts of your father ye will do. He was a murderer from the beginning, and abode not in the truth, because there is no truth in him. When he speaketh a lie, he speaketh of his own: for he is a liar, and the father of it. And because I tell you the truth, ye believe me not. Which of you convinceth me of sin? And if I say the truth, why do ye not believe me? He that is of God heareth God's words: ye therefore hear them not, because ye are not of God. Then answered the Jews, and said unto him, Say we not well that thou art a Samaritan, and hast a devil? (John 8:42–48, emphasis added)

Jesus said to the religious leaders, "Ye are of your father the devil." Their father was the devil because they inherited the devil's distorted picture of God and resisted any change to that picture.

And set up over his head his accusation written, THIS IS JESUS THE KING OF THE JEWS. Then were there two thieves crucified with him, one on the right hand, and another on the left. And they that passed by reviled him, wagging their heads, And saying, Thou that destroyest the temple, and buildest it in three days, save thyself. *If thou be the Son of God,* come down from the cross. Likewise also the chief priests mocking him, with the scribes and elders, said, He saved others; himself he cannot save. *If he be the King of Israel,* let him now come down from the cross, and we will believe him. He trusted in God; let him deliver him now, *if he will have him*: for he said, I am the Son of God. (Matt. 27:37–43, emphasis added)

Those who mocked Jesus at the cross used the very same insinuation that Satan used in the wilderness to tempt Christ: "If thou be the Son of God" (Matt. 4:3).

And no man putteth new wine into old bottles; else the new wine will burst the bottles, and be spilled, and the bottles shall perish. But new wine must be put into new bottles; and both are preserved. (Luke 5:37–38)

Jesus, in this analogy, likens his radical new teaching to "new wine" bursting "old bottles." Jesus by word and example painted a clear picture of God's love that stood in sharp contrast to the *distorted picture of God* (the "old wine") held by the religious teachers (the "old bottles") he encountered. These two contrasting views could not be mixed together. So it is today. The picture of a violent god must go to make room for our gentle God in our minds.

12

How God Destroys

One of the clearest examples of *how* God destroys is found in the book of 1 Chronicles. Saul the king of Israel had been disregarding God's counsel, communicated to him through the prophet Samuel, to turn from his destructive course. Saul had made several attempts to kill David, his loyal servant. He was also guilty of having the priests of Nob killed, and he had taken counsel of a witch. Saul had been wounded in a battle with the Philistines, and he was terrified of what would happen if he was captured. In his desperation, "Saul took a sword, and fell upon it" (1 Chron. 10:4).

Notice how the Bible concludes this tragic account of Saul's death:

> So Saul died for his transgression which he committed against the LORD, even against the word of the LORD, which he kept not, and also for asking counsel of one that had a familiar spirit, to inquire of it; And inquired not of the LORD: therefore he slew him, and turned the kingdom unto David the son of Jesse. (1 Chron. 10:13–14)

It is evident that in Saul's death the only *action* we see God taking is to let Saul go his own way and experience the consequences of his actions. Saul's cause of death was suicide, not homicide, and yet the Bible states that God *slew* him. The

40

word used here to describe what God did is decidedly different from the dictionary definition. This is not an isolated example. In the next chapter, words in the Bible such as anger, wrath, and jealously will be examined. Scripture gives these words an entirely different meaning from their common usage when referring to God's ways and God's thoughts.

Seek ye the LORD while he may be found, call ye upon him while he is near: Let the wicked forsake his way, and the unrighteous man his thoughts: and let him return unto the LORD, and he will have mercy upon him; and to our God, for he will abundantly pardon. For my thoughts are not your thoughts, neither are your ways my ways, saith the LORD. For as the heavens are higher than the earth, so are my ways higher than your ways, and my thoughts than your thoughts.

—Isaiah 55:6–9

13

What Is God's Anger?

The question of God's anger perplexes many of us when we read the Old Testament. There are many references to God's anger and wrath, but what *is* his anger? To answer this question, it will be enlightening to look at some examples in the Bible. The first mention of God's anger was when he commissioned Moses to lead the children of Israel from Egyptian bondage to freedom. What were the circumstances that compelled God to manifest his anger at that time?

> And Moses said unto the LORD, O my Lord, I am not eloquent, neither heretofore, nor since thou hast spoken unto thy servant: but I am slow of speech, and of a slow tongue. And the LORD said unto him, Who hath made man's mouth? ... have not I the LORD? Now therefore go, and I will be with thy mouth, and teach thee what thou shalt say. And he said, O my Lord, send, I pray thee, by the hand of him whom thou wilt send. (Ex. 4:10–13)

Moses was fearful of going in before Pharaoh alone and requested a spokesman. How did God respond?

> And the anger of the LORD was kindled against Moses, and he said, Is not Aaron the Levite thy brother? I know that he can speak well. And

also, behold, he cometh forth to meet thee: and when he seeth thee, he will be glad in his heart. (Ex. 4:14)

How did God express his anger? By giving Moses what he wanted. Let's look at some other Bible passages with references to God's anger:

> And the mixt multitude that was among them fell a lusting: and the children of Israel also wept again, and said, Who shall give us flesh to eat? Then Moses heard the people weep throughout their families, every man in the door of his tent: and the anger of the LORD was kindled greatly; Moses also was displeased. And there went forth a wind from the LORD, and brought quails from the sea, and let them fall by the camp, as it were a day's journey on this side, and as it were a day's journey on the other side, round about the camp, and as it were two cubits high upon the face of the earth. And the people stood up all that day, and all that night, and all the next day, and they gathered the quails: he that gathered least gathered ten homers: and they spread them all abroad for themselves round about the camp. (Num. 11:4, 10, 31–32)

In this incident, we again find God's anger mentioned. What did he do? He gave the people what they wanted.

> And it came to pass, when Samuel was old, that he made his sons judges over Israel. Now

the name of his firstborn was Joel; and the name of his second, Abiah: they were judges in Beersheba. And his sons walked not in his ways, but turned aside after lucre, and took bribes, and perverted judgment. Then all the elders of Israel gathered themselves together, and came to Samuel unto Ramah, And said unto him, Behold, thou art old, and thy sons walk not in thy ways: now make us a king to judge us like all the nations. But the thing displeased Samuel, when they said, Give us a king to judge us. And Samuel prayed unto the LORD. And the LORD said unto Samuel, Hearken unto the voice of the people in all that they say unto thee: for they have not rejected thee, but they have rejected me, that I should not reign over them. (1 Sam. 8:1–7)

God sent a message to the people through his prophet Samuel giving many reasons why it would *not* be in their best interest for him to grant their request for a king. Did they listen to Samuel?

Nevertheless the people refused to obey the voice of Samuel; and they said, Nay; but we will have a king over us; That we also may be like all the nations; and that our king may judge us, and go out before us, and fight our battles. (1 Sam. 8:19–20)

How did God respond to the people's insistence? "And the LORD said to Samuel, Hearken unto their voice, and make them a king" (v. 22). How do we know that God gave them a king in anger? The prophet Hosea, looking back on this historical event, gives us God's perspective on the role he played in granting the people's request:

> O Israel, thou hast destroyed thyself; but in me is thine help. I will be thy king: where is any other that may save thee in all thy cities? and thy judges of whom thou saidst, Give me a king and princes? *I gave thee a king in mine anger, and took him away in my wrath.* (Hos. 13:9–11, emphasis added)

These three scriptural accounts clearly show that God's anger was synonymous with him giving the Israelite people what they wanted when it was not in their best interest for him to do so. This should be enough, at the very least, to suggest that God's anger can be defined, from the Bible, as something decidedly different from the definition found in the dictionary. However, there is much more than this. What happened when Jesus got angry?

> And he entered again into the synagogue; and there was a man there which had a withered hand. And they watched him, whether he would heal him on the sabbath day; that they might accuse him. And he saith unto the man which had the withered hand, Stand forth. And he saith unto them, Is it lawful to do good on the sabbath days, or to do evil? to save life, or to kill? But they held their peace. And when he had looked round about on them with anger, being grieved for the hardness of their hearts, he saith unto the man, Stretch forth thine

hand. And he stretched it out: and his hand was restored whole as the other. And the Pharisees went forth, and straightway took counsel with the Herodians against him, how they might destroy him. (Mark 3:1–6)

This is an encounter Jesus had with the Pharisees. Their legalistic restrictions prohibited healing on the Sabbath day. Jesus, reading their hearts, "looked round about on them with anger." What kind of anger did Jesus have? The kind that is described as "being grieved for the hardness of their hearts." Jesus was experiencing grief or deep sadness at the lack of love and sympathy demonstrated by these pitiless religious leaders for the man with the withered hand. What more can we discover in the Bible about God's anger and wrath?

For the *wrath of God is revealed* from heaven against all ungodliness and unrighteousness of men, who hold the truth in unrighteousness. (Rom. 1:18, emphasis added)

How is the wrath of God revealed?

Wherefore *God also gave them up* to uncleanness through the lusts of their own hearts. (Rom. 1:24, emphasis added)

For this cause *God gave them up* unto vile affections. (Rom. 1:26, emphasis added)

And even as they did not like to retain God in their knowledge, *God gave them over* to a reprobate mind. (Rom. 1:28, emphasis added)

God's *wrath* is defined here as God *giving them up* or *giving them over*—in other words, God is giving the people freedom to separate from himself. Not exactly the wrath of revengeful destruction we often credit to God's account. Let's look at some more Old Testament passages.

> And the people stood up all that day, and all that night, and all the next day, and they gathered the quails: he that gathered least gathered ten homers: and they spread them all abroad for themselves round about the camp. And while the flesh was yet between their teeth, ere it was chewed, the wrath of the LORD was kindled against the people, and the LORD smote the people with a very great plague. (Num. 11:32–33)

We return here to the account of the quails God gave to the people in anger. There was a natural consequence resulting from the people's gluttony: "the LORD smote the people with a very great plague."

It is worth noting that tons of fresh quail meat would not last long in the desert environment where the Israelites were encamped. The meat would quickly spoil making it unfit for human consumption. Considering this fact, what kind of plague would likely have resulted? Given the right microbe and the right conditions, food poisoning is a deadly affliction: "And he called the name of that place Kibrothhattaavah [graves of lust]: because there they buried the people that lusted" (v. 34). What was "the wrath of the LORD"? Doesn't it reasonably follow that God's wrath was his *nonintervention* in a cause and effect event?

Then my anger shall be kindled against them in that day, and I will forsake them, and I will hide my face from them, and they shall be devoured, and many evils and troubles shall befall them; so that they will say in that day, Are not these evils come upon us, because our God is not among us? And I will surely hide my face in that day for all the evils which they shall have wrought, in that they are turned unto other gods. (Deut. 31:17–18)

What does it mean when God *hides his face*? "Are not these evils come upon us, because our God is *not* among us?" This again is language that describes God's nonintervention. Why did God say he would hide his face? "For all the evils which they shall have wrought, in that they are turned unto other gods." And what would be the result? "They shall be devoured, and many evils and troubles shall befall them." When the people turned to other gods, they turned away from the true God, and he was unable to shield them from the inevitable consequences.

And the children of Israel did evil in the sight of the LORD, and served Baalim: And they forsook the LORD God of their fathers, which brought them out of the land of Egypt, and followed other gods, of the gods of the people that were round about them, and bowed themselves unto them, and provoked the LORD to anger. And they forsook the LORD, and served Baal and Ashtaroth. And the anger of the LORD was hot against Israel, and he delivered them into the hands of spoilers that spoiled them, and he sold them into the hands of their enemies round about, so that they could not any longer stand before their enemies. (Judg. 2:11–14)

This passage describes the people's continuing apostasy from the Lord. Here God "delivered them into the hands of spoilers" and "sold them into the hands of their enemies." This is again a passive response to the crisis. Because of their apostasy, God was unable to prevent Israel's enemies from invading their lands.

> For the LORD shall smite Israel, as a reed is shaken in the water, and he shall root up Israel out of this good land, which he gave to their fathers, and shall scatter them beyond the river, because they have made their groves, provoking the LORD to anger. And he shall give Israel up because of the sins of Jeroboam, who did sin, and who made Israel to sin. (1 Kings 14:15–16)

Here God's anger (and smiting) is *giving up* apostate Israel.

> For they provoked him to anger with their high places, and moved him to jealousy with their graven images. When God heard this, he was wroth, and greatly abhorred Israel: So that he forsook the tabernacle of Shiloh, the tent which he placed among men; And delivered his strength into captivity, and his glory into the enemy's hand. He gave his people over also unto the sword; and was wroth with his inheritance. (Ps. 78:58–62)

Here the definition of wrath includes: *forsaking, delivering into captivity*, and *giving over.*

> Therefore was the wrath of the LORD kindled against his people, insomuch that he abhorred his own inheritance. And he gave them into the hand of the heathen; and they that hated them ruled over them. (Ps. 106:40–41)

God's wrath is described here as giving "them into the hand of the heathen."

> In a little wrath I hid my face from thee for a moment; but with everlasting kindness will I have mercy on thee, saith the LORD thy Redeemer. (Isa. 54:8)

In this passage, "a little wrath" is defined as God hiding his face "for a moment," but God's kindness and mercy toward us is everlasting.

> And I will cast you out of my sight, as I have cast out all your brethren, even the whole seed of Ephraim. Do they provoke me to anger? saith the LORD: do they not provoke themselves to the confusion of their own faces? Therefore thus saith the Lord GOD; Behold, mine anger and my fury shall be poured out upon this place, upon man, and upon beast, and upon the trees of the field, and upon the fruit of the ground; and it shall burn, and shall not be quenched. (Jer. 7:15, 19–20)

God asks, "Do they provoke me to anger? ... do they not provoke themselves to the confusion of their own faces?" The people's troubles were brought about as a *consequence* of their idolatry not as punishment from God.

> Cut off thine hair, O Jerusalem, and cast it away, and take up a lamentation on high places; for the LORD hath rejected and *forsaken the generation of his wrath*. (Jer. 7:29, emphasis added)

There are more Bible passages that use similar terminology, but these we have looked at should suffice to make a compelling case that God's wrath is *never* punishment from him. God gives us freedom to accept him or reject him. God's wrath is the natural consequences of our wrong choices, when he is compelled to let us have our own way. God's role is always a passive one referred to as *forsaking, hiding his face, giving over, letting go, delivering* and similar terminology.

In his proclamation before Moses, God did not list *wrath* or *anger* as attributes of his character: "And the LORD passed by before him, and proclaimed, The LORD, The LORD God, merciful and gracious, longsuffering, and abundant in goodness and truth, Keeping mercy for thousands, forgiving iniquity and transgression and sin" (Ex. 34:6–7).

> And the people spake against God, and against Moses, Wherefore have ye brought us up out of Egypt to die in the wilderness? for there is no bread, neither is there any water; and our soul loatheth this light bread. And the LORD sent fiery serpents among the people, and they bit the people; and much people of Israel died. (Num. 21:5–6)

This passage informs us that "the LORD sent fiery serpents among the people" in response to their complaints. From the scriptural evidence we have looked at so far, what would God's action have been when he "sent" the serpents? In harmony with the other Bible passages we have examined, God was compelled by the people's rebellious ingratitude to give them freedom *from* his protective intervention on their behalf.

How did the fiery serpents come to be there in the first place? "[The LORD thy God] who led thee through that great and terrible wilderness, *wherein were fiery serpents*, and scorpions, and drought, where there was no water; who brought thee forth water out of the rock of flint" (Deut. 8:15, emphasis added).

The fiery serpents were there all along as one of many hazards God miraculously protected the Israelites from in that harsh desert environment. This account of God sending the fiery serpents would only be problematic if God had sent hungry polar bears instead.

There are many accounts in the Bible of God sending invading armies or some calamity against the people. With this understanding, we can reasonably conclude that in every scriptural account where God *sent* something harmful, it means that God was unable to prevent it from occurring without being a manipulator of cause and effect events. It is not God's purpose, nor is it within his nature, to exercise control over human affairs.

> Then will the LORD be jealous for his land, and pity his people. Yea, the LORD will answer and say unto his people, Behold, I will send you corn, and wine, and oil, and ye shall be satisfied

therewith: and I will no more make you a reproach among the heathen. (Joel 2:18–19)

So the angel that communed with me said unto me, Cry thou, saying, Thus saith the LORD of hosts; I am jealous for Jerusalem and for Zion with a great jealousy. (Zech. 1:14)

For I am jealous over you with godly jealousy: for I have espoused you to one husband, that I may present you as a chaste virgin to Christ. But I fear, lest by any means, as the serpent beguiled Eve through his subtilty, so your minds should be corrupted from the simplicity that is in Christ. (2 Cor. 11:2–3)

God's jealousy is completely unselfish. God is jealous for others, never for himself.

And again the anger of the LORD was kindled against Israel, and he moved David against them to say, Go, number Israel and Judah. For the king said to Joab the captain of the host, which was with him, Go now through all the tribes of Israel, from Dan even to Beersheba, and number ye the people, that I may know the number of the people. And Joab said unto the king, Now the LORD thy God add unto the people, how many soever they be, an hundredfold, and that the eyes of my lord the king may see it: but why doth my lord the king delight in this thing? Notwithstanding the king's word prevailed against Joab, and against the captains of the host. And Joab and the captains of the host went out from the presence of the king, to number the people of Israel. (2 Sam. 24:1–4)

When David numbered Israel he was demonstrating pride and distrust in God by looking to human numbers and military might to protect Israel. This effectively excluded God's nonviolent protection over them, leaving them vulnerable to their enemies and other threats. Even battle-hardened Joab saw danger in the king's request to number Israel and questioned him about it.

God "moved David against them." Could there be a problem understanding this statement just as it reads? Was God whispering in David's ear to number Israel so he would have a good excuse to turn against them? Let's look at this verse in the light of what we have learned so far about God's actions.

God doesn't take an active role in destruction, and he doesn't stir up evil, but there is someone who does. Is it possible, in this incident, that God "moved" David to number Israel by not preventing him from doing so? And would it be going too far to suggest that it wasn't God whispering in David's ear but Satan? How can we know? We can read about this same incident in the book of 1 Chronicles: "And *Satan* stood up against Israel, and *provoked* David to number Israel" (1 Chron. 21:1, emphasis added).

We might wonder why the Bible doesn't just come right out and say exactly what took place in every encounter within its pages; wouldn't that make Bible study much simpler? Yes, it would. However, the communication problem between God and humankind has never been because of God's lack of understanding, but because of ours. God, in his wisdom, gives us the choice to either accept or reject the truth about him. The Bible was written with this important principle in mind. When we have the opportunity to understand saving truth about God and we reject it, more light will only drive us further from him. The Bible's surface ambiguity allows for opposing interpretations for that reason. It is not in God's character to convince us, against our will, to believe in him and his uncompromising love. At the same time, the Bible provides abundant evidence for those who *are* looking for our gentle God to find him.

And ye shall seek me, and find me, when ye shall search for me with all your heart.

—Jeremiah 29:13

14

How God Wages War

God wages war against evil with truth, love, mercy, and forgiveness.

> He that committeth sin is of the devil; for the devil sinneth from the beginning. For this purpose the Son of God was manifested, that he might destroy the works of the devil. (1 John 3:8)

The devil's work from the beginning of his rebellion has been to accuse and misrepresent God. Jesus, God the Son, destroyed the devil's work by demonstrating that his accusations against God were a lie.

> Why do ye not understand my speech? even because ye cannot hear my word. Ye are of your father the devil, and the lusts of your father ye will do. He was a murderer from the beginning, and abode not in the truth, because there is no truth in him. When he speaketh a lie, he speaketh of his own: for he is a liar, and the father of it. (John 8:43–44)

Jesus affirms that the devil's primary weapon is his use of lies. It is "impossible for God to lie" (Heb. 6:18); he combats the devil's lies with truth.

> Put on the whole armour of God, that ye may
> be able to stand against the wiles of the devil.
> For we wrestle not against flesh and blood, but
> against principalities, against powers, against
> the rulers of the darkness of this world, against
> spiritual wickedness in high places. Wherefore
> take unto you the whole armour of God, that
> ye may be able to withstand in the evil day,
> and having done all, to stand. Stand therefore,
> having your loins girt about with truth, and
> having on the breastplate of righteousness;
> And your feet shod with the preparation of the
> gospel of peace; Above all, taking the shield
> of faith, wherewith ye shall be able to quench
> all the fiery darts of the wicked. And take the
> helmet of salvation, and the sword of the Spirit,
> which is the word of God. (Eph. 6:11–17)

Jesus demonstrated for us the use of the armor of God: the good news of the truth about God ("your loins girt about with truth"), his fulfillment of covenantal faithfulness ("the breastplate of righteousness"), the message of reconciliation to our Heavenly Father ("the gospel of peace"), the assurance of God's trustworthiness ("the shield of faith"), and the promise of eternal life to those freed from bondage to Satan and his lies ("the helmet of salvation"). We are also encouraged to take up the same weapon Jesus used—God's Word ("the sword of the Spirit").

> Dearly beloved, avenge not yourselves, but rather
> give place unto wrath: for it is written, Vengeance
> is mine; I will repay, saith the Lord. Therefore if
> thine enemy hunger, feed him; if he thirst, give
> him drink: for in so doing thou shalt heap coals

of fire on his head. Be not overcome of evil, but overcome evil with good. (Rom. 12:19–21)

What *is* God's vengeance? He overcomes evil with good, and he invites his children to do the same. Treating our enemies with kindness rather than with retaliation is likened to heaping "coals of fire" on their heads. To retaliate against an enemy is to be overcome by evil. However, there *is* a way to effectively overcome evil—"with good." That's God's way of doing battle.

Then said Jesus, Father, forgive them; for they know not what they do. (Luke 23:34)

These words of Jesus are for our benefit. The Father does not need any persuasion to forgive. The problem is not with God, but with us. We think that God is like us. When Jesus spoke the words, "Father, forgive them; for they know not what they do," he was speaking not only on behalf of those who hung him on the cross; he was speaking on *our* behalf as well. God wants us to know that he understands our predicament (we don't know what we are doing); he still loves us unconditionally and is working tirelessly to save us.

But the fruit of the Spirit is love, joy, peace, longsuffering, gentleness, goodness, faith, Meekness, temperance: against such there is no law.

—Galatians 5:22-23

15

Sodom and Gomorrah

The destruction of Sodom and Gomorrah is thought of as the classic example of an angry God raining down death and destruction on a wicked people. If we take the account in the Bible just as it reads, isolated from the larger scriptural context, what appears to happen is the following: The two cities are situated in a prosperous agricultural and trade area, and life becomes relatively easy for the inhabitants. The people have a good deal of leisure time and ungodly activities become commonplace. God looks down from heaven and is angered by the extent of their wickedness. He refrains from taking any action for a while, but the depravity finally becomes so bad that God's patience is exhausted. He sends a warning to righteous Lot and his family to leave Sodom. Then, in a spectacular display of wrath, God rains down fire and brimstone out of heaven. Men, women, and children meet a horrible death. Sodom and Gomorrah are annihilated, and God's vengeance is satisfied.

Now, let's take another look at this same event with the understanding that God does not take an active role in destruction. Picture the two cities with the self-serving inhabitants enjoying their prosperity and pleasures: "Behold, this was the iniquity of thy sister Sodom, pride, fulness of bread, and abundance of idleness was in her and in her daughters, neither did she strengthen the hand of the poor and needy" (Ezek. 16:49). The people are unaware that beneath their cities (which are built in a geologically unstable area) volcanic forces are building; fissures containing molten rock push upward. They are also unaware that the invisible God, whom they are rejecting, is also the same God who has, up to this point in time, protected them from calamity. The day finally arrives when God must acknowledge their desire for independence from him. To uphold their freedom, he reluctantly *lets* them go, leaving them unshielded from the forces of nature out of his control. The fissures beneath the earth's surface rip upward spewing molten rock thousands of feet into the air and raining down "brimstone and fire from the LORD out of heaven" (Gen. 19:24), destroying Sodom and Gomorrah in a matter of minutes.

God's *act* in destroying the two cities was giving the inhabitants genuine freedom—including the freedom to make choices with catastrophic consequences: "I call heaven and earth to record this day against you, that I have set before you life and death, blessing and cursing: therefore choose life, that both thou and thy seed may live: That thou mayest love the LORD thy God, and that thou mayest obey his voice, and that thou mayest cleave unto him: for he is thy life, and the length of thy days" (Deut. 30:19–20).

Sickness, accidents, death, wars, natural disasters, and so forth occur for many reasons. Often *we* are directly responsible, sometimes Satan is, and sometimes the postdiluvian forces of nature are to blame. More often some combination of contributing factors is involved. Because we can't see clearly *why* a particular instance of suffering took place, we are inclined to blame God for it. Is that fair? Is it reasonable? Our propensity to shift blame has been around a long time. When and where did this evasion of responsibility begin? "And the man said, The *woman* whom *thou* gavest to be with me, *she* gave me of the tree, and I did eat. And the LORD God said unto the woman, What is this that thou hast done? And the woman said, *The serpent* beguiled me, and I did eat" (Gen. 3:12–13, emphasis added).

Thy mercy, O LORD, is in the heavens; and thy faithfulness reacheth unto the clouds. Thy righteousness is like the great mountains; thy judgments are a great deep: O LORD, thou preservest man and beast. How excellent is thy lovingkindness, O God! therefore the children of men put their trust under the shadow of thy wings. Thy mercy, O LORD, is in the heavens; and thy faithfulness reacheth unto the clouds.
—Psalm 36:5-7

16

What about the Flood?

What about the flood of Noah's day? If God is not the destroyer, what took place to bring about our world's largest cataclysm? What evidence can we find in the Bible and elsewhere to give us a reasonable explanation for what caused this massive worldwide flood?

> And the LORD said, My spirit shall not always strive with man, for that he also is flesh: yet his days shall be an hundred and twenty years. (Gen. 6:3)

God was apparently looking ahead to a time when humankind would distance themselves so far from him that he would be compelled to let them go by loosening his sustaining hold on the forces of nature. We might wonder what finally prompted him to let go. Did God make a calculated decision to do so, or was another factor involved?

Imagine you have a neighbor who has a number of personal problems. He struggles financially, has several health issues, and is unable to walk more than a few blocks from home. On top of that, he doesn't own a car, making it difficult for him to run errands and get his needs met.

One day, in conversation with him, you learn of his lack of transportation and offer to drive him to the grocery store and other locations. Over the next few months, you give him rides in your car to doctor's appointments, the pharmacy, and the supermarket. This arrangement seems to be working well, and you are glad to help him.

Then one warm summer day this same neighbor shows up at your door in what appears to be an agitated frame of mind and asks you to drive him to a bank across town. You notice he is carrying a paper bag, a ski mask, and what looks like a handgun wrapped in a sock. What would you do? Would you grab your car keys and cheerfully rush out the door to chauffeur your friend to his destination and back?

All of us have lines we are not willing to cross. These lines pertain to moral, ethical, and personal boundary issues. Isn't it reasonable to believe that God also has lines *he* won't cross— or *can't?*

> And God saw that the wickedness of man was great in the earth, and that every imagination of the thoughts of his heart was only evil continually. The earth also was corrupt before God, and the earth was filled with violence. And God looked upon the earth, and, behold, it was corrupt; for all flesh had corrupted his way upon the earth. And God said unto Noah, The end of all flesh is come before me; for the earth is filled with violence through them; and, behold, I will destroy them with the earth. (Gen. 6:5, 11–13)

What was our world like just prior to the flood? God revealed to Noah, "the earth was filled with violence *through them*" (v 13, emphasis added). Because of humankind's violence, the earth itself had been *storing up* violence. Extraordinarily violent forces were soon to be unleashed in the coming cataclysm. Human society was in moral collapse:

"And God looked upon the earth, and, behold, it was corrupt; for all flesh had corrupted his way upon the earth."

How many loyal followers did God have during this particularly dark time in history? Noah alone is mentioned in the Bible. What brought about this sad state of affairs? Humankind's thoughts were "only evil continually." How does the Bible define evil? When Adam and Eve ate the fruit of the "tree of the knowledge of good and evil" (Gen. 2:17), their change of mind about God's goodness perfectly defines *what evil is*. Our first parents' distorted picture of our gentle God is what the world inherited. The violent inhabitants of the antediluvian world imagined that God condoned their violence. What was God's response? "It grieved him at his heart" (Gen. 6:6).

Humankind had pushed God right up to the line he *couldn't* cross without becoming an involuntary participant in the violence himself. God was compelled to loosen his hold on the natural world. When the 120-year period had ended, and the passengers were safely in the ark, the rain began to fall, pouring down torrents for forty days and forty nights. What triggered this massive deluge? We find important clues in the first chapter of Genesis:

> And God said, Let there be a firmament in the midst of the waters, and let it divide the waters from the waters. And God made the firmament, and divided the waters which were under the firmament from the waters which were above the firmament: and it was so. And God called the firmament Heaven. (Gen. 1:6–8)

What is a firmament? Firmament means an expanse, a vault, or a dome. A dome refers to a covering over the earth suspended or fixed in the heaven or atmosphere. The passage goes on to describe this dome as separating the waters, with a significant amount of water *above* the dome.

A massive covering of atmospheric water vapor encircled the entire earth like a gigantic greenhouse giving our world an even and mild tropical climate from the North Pole to the South Pole. Fossilized remains of warm-climate plants and animals have been found in polar regions giving evidence that such a climate once existed on our planet. The Bible also gives another important clue about the climate of the earth in those early days:

> These are the generations of the heavens and of the earth when they were created, in the day that the LORD God made the earth and the heavens, And every plant of the field before it was in the earth, and every herb of the field before it grew: for the LORD God had not caused it to rain upon the earth, ... But there went up a mist from the earth, and watered the whole face of the ground. (Gen. 2:4–6)

These verses suggest a world very different from the one we are familiar with today. "The LORD God had not caused it to rain upon the earth ... But there went up a mist from the earth, and watered the whole face of the ground." The earth had a moist yet warm and exceptionally even climate, with no abrupt temperature changes. With such even temperatures there would have been no thunderstorms, no tornadoes, no hurricanes, no hail, or snow, and apparently not even rain. It is also likely that the surface of the earth itself was much more level than it is today, with no towering mountains or deep sea canyons. In addition, much less of the earth's surface would have been covered with water.

What kept all the water suspended in the atmosphere, and what was the mechanism that triggered the deluge to begin? We know from simple observation that heat causes water to rise. Water heated in a kettle on the stove escapes out of the spout as evaporation. Bodies of water on our planet give up a massive volume of water molecules every day. The more heat that is applied, the faster they escape. Relatively few water molecules evaporate from the surface of a frozen lake in midwinter compared to a hot summer day.

What if there was more heat energy available before the flood; wouldn't that have supported more water in the atmosphere? Our earth gets virtually all of its heat energy from our sun. Without it our world would become ultra-frozen with a surface temperature approaching absolute zero.

When God created our world, he put into operation an amazingly precise heat-energy system able to suspend a massive quantity of water in the atmosphere. The sun would have been a key mechanism in the operation of this system. It is also reasonable to believe that the sun before the flood put out *more* heat than it does today. If this is true, then it is reasonable to believe that when God was compelled to loosen his hold on the natural world the sun's energy output would have been affected.

The delicate balance in the atmosphere was disrupted, and "In the six hundredth year of Noah's life, in the second month, the seventeenth day of the month, the same day were all the fountains of the deep broken up, and the windows of heaven were opened. And the rain was upon the earth forty days and forty nights" (Gen. 7:11–12). History's first raindrops began falling, eventually pouring down thousands of cubic miles of water on the earth.

Geological instability coincided with the atmospheric instability causing increased water pressure in underground reservoirs: "The same day were all the fountains of the great deep broken up" (Gen. 7:11). These "fountains" contributed much additional flood water.

Only the eight people in the ark survived the flood: Noah and his family. Numerous animal species were also aboard the massive ship for the purpose of repopulating the world with each kind of animal after the flood.

The fossilized remains of the ark are preserved in a national park dedicated to the site of the ark in Eastern Turkey, near the small city of Dogubayazit. This extraordinary archaeological discovery, in the mountains of Ararat, is compelling evidence that the Biblical account of the great flood is *not* a fable, but reliable history of the only worldwide natural disaster:

And the waters returned from off the earth continually: and after the end of the hundred and fifty days the waters were abated. And the ark rested in the seventh month, on the seventeenth day of the month, upon the mountains of Ararat.

—Genesis 8:3–4

17

The Testimony of the Cross

By a correct understanding of God's actions in the Old Testament, we are assured that he does not destroy—regardless of circumstances. However, the most compelling evidence that God does not come near the sinner to destroy him is found in the New Testament.

The belief that Jesus died for us on the cross is nearly universal among Bible students, although there are differing views as to how the death of Jesus saves us. Nevertheless, most believe that when Jesus died on the cross, he experienced what we are destined to experience without his self-sacrificing intervention on our behalf.

If this is true, then we would expect to find that Jesus died the same way we would have to die in relation to what God "does" to bring about death. If we believe it is God who destroys the sinner, then we would also expect that God the Father came near to Jesus to kill him. Is this what we find? The gospel of Matthew gives a detailed account of the crucifixion of Christ. What were Jesus's last words just moments before his death? "My God, my God, why hast thou *forsaken* me?" (Matt. 27:46, emphasis added).

This verse reveals how Jesus died. God the Father allowed his Son to experience what every person who rejects his love will experience in the end—separation from him, the Life-Giver. God the Father did not kill Jesus—our sin did: "The wages of sin is death" (Rom. 6:23). Sin is perfectly capable of causing death all by itself, without any help from God. All life is from God with no exceptions. All death is the consequence of sin with no exceptions. To imagine that God is the source of death is *illogical*—with no exceptions.

It is not possible in this small volume to examine every account of destruction and suffering that are attributed to God. However, the passages we have examined are a key to a correct understanding of God's role in death and disasters in the Bible. The Bible interprets the Bible. When scripture pulls back the curtain in a particular passage to make clear what God's actions are, we can use that as a key to understand other passages that are not as clear (as when two Bible passages seem to contradict each other). In addition, the words of God about himself are worthy of special consideration, for example: "I am the LORD, I change not" (Mal. 3:6). Finally, the truth about God, that Jesus taught and demonstrated, is an accurate roadmap for navigating the entire Bible from Genesis to Revelation.

That Christ may dwell in your hearts by faith;
that ye, being rooted and grounded in love,
May be able to comprehend with all saints
what is the breadth, and length, and depth,
and height; And to know the love of Christ,
which passeth knowledge, that ye might be
filled with all the fulness of God.
—Ephesians 3:17–19

18

God Is Not a Tyrant

There is wonderful news for everyone who has been exposed to the doctrine of an eternally burning hell. This doctrine is not supported by a thorough study of the Bible. Scripture describes death as an unconscious state. It is a temporary *sleep* that will last only until the resurrection. After that time, all who have resisted reconciliation to God will reap, as the natural consequence, eternal nonexistence.

To find support for an ever-burning place of torment in the Bible, we must do so by literalizing words that are meant to be symbolic. The word *fire* can have either a literal or a symbolic meaning. In the book of Daniel, when Nebuchadnezzar had Shadrach, Meshach, and Abednego thrown into the burning fiery furnace, it was obviously a literal fire they experienced. When John the Baptist, who baptized with water, said Christ would baptize with the Holy Spirit and with fire, he was obviously *not* referring to literal fire, but was using the word *fire* figuratively.

"Our God is a consuming fire," and "God is love" (Heb. 12:29, 1 John 4:16). Are these two definitive statements about God in conflict? Only if we think of the fire as a literal fire. Fire is a chemical reaction. Is God a chemical reaction? These statements are in perfect harmony if we understand the effect that God's love has on a person. God's love consumes selfishness. Selfishness is the opposite of genuine love. If we are open to God's love, that same love will come into us consuming the deadly selfishness in our hearts. This is a life-giving experience.

If we resist God's love, clinging instead to our own selfishness, that same love will be a source of torment. We will seek to move away from it and even flee or hide from God. That was the experience of Adam and Eve after they believed the serpent's lie about God. Understood in this way, we can see that God's love *is* the consuming fire.

Jesus's parable of the rich man and Lazarus is sometimes used to support the doctrine of a literal place of torment:

> There was a certain rich man, which was clothed in purple and fine linen, and fared sumptuously every day: And there was a certain beggar named Lazarus, which was laid at his gate, full of sores, And desiring to be fed with the crumbs which fell from the rich man's table: moreover the dogs came and licked his sores. And it came to pass, that the beggar died, and was carried by the angels into Abraham's bosom: the rich man also died, and was buried; And in hell he lift up his eyes, being in torments, and seeth Abraham afar off, and Lazarus in his bosom. And he cried and said, Father Abraham, have mercy on me, and send Lazarus, that he may dip the tip of his finger in water, and cool my tongue; for I am tormented in this flame. But Abraham said, Son, remember that thou in thy lifetime receivedst thy good things, and likewise Lazarus evil things: but now he is comforted, and thou art tormented. And beside all this, between us and you there is a great gulf fixed: so

that they which would pass from hence to you cannot; neither can they pass to us, that would come from thence. Then he said, I pray thee therefore, father, that thou wouldest send him to my father's house: For I have five brethren; that he may testify unto them, lest they also come into this place of torment. Abraham saith unto him, They have Moses and the prophets; let them hear them. And he said, Nay, father Abraham: but if one went unto them from the dead, they will repent. And he said unto him, If they hear not Moses and the prophets, neither will they be persuaded, though one rose from the dead. (Luke 16:19–31)

Jesus told this parable to illustrate the effect that selfishness and indifference has on a person. Jesus was addressing self-righteous Pharisees, and he wrapped his parable around commonly held misconceptions about the afterlife.

The Jews associated wealth with the blessing of God. In their minds a poor person, especially one who had some physical affliction, was cursed by God; the thought being that the person deserved his or her lot in life because of some spiritual deficiency or sin. The rich person, on the other hand, was assured of God's special favor. A person's wealth or status was, to the Pharisees' way of thinking, a measure of their right standing before God. Jesus gave them this parable to expose the fallacy of this narrow and cruel perspective.

First we will look at a few story details. After his death, Lazarus, the beggar, finds himself comfortably situated in "Abraham's bosom." The rich man also dies and ends up in hell suffering torment; he looks up and sees Abraham and Lazarus at a distance. A conversation follows between the rich man and "Father Abraham."

Now let's carefully examine this story by asking some thoughtful questions:

- Where are Abraham and Lazarus located in the story?
- If Abraham and Lazarus are in heaven or paradise, how is it possible that Abraham can carry on a conversation with the rich man who is in hell, and how is it possible for the rich man to see them?
- If Abraham and Lazarus are in hell, what are they doing there?
- If Abraham and Lazarus are in neither heaven nor hell, where are they?
- How much relief would a few drops of water on the tongue provide to a person being tormented in a fiery hell?
- Can Lazarus see the rich man being tormented in hell and hear his pleas?
- How is Lazarus being comforted in Abraham's bosom?
- Is Lazarus comforted *despite* his apparent awareness of the rich man's suffering or *because* of it?
- Is Lazarus being encouraged to foster a callous indifference toward the rich man now that their situations are reversed?
- How wide is the "great gulf" that prevents travel between the two locations?
- How wide would this great gulf need to be to prevent communication between hell and the location of Abraham and Lazarus?
- How wide would this great gulf need to be to prevent awareness of the suffering of those being tormented

in hell by those who are located on the comfortable side of the gulf? Three hundred yards? Three hundred miles? Would the universe be wide enough?

- Is it reasonable to conclude that because Jesus used a reference to hell in the parable of the rich man and Lazarus that he was lending support to the doctrine of an eternally burning hell?

Doesn't it seem *more* reasonable to conclude that Jesus brought the concept of an ever-burning place of torment into his parable to dispel this monstrous doctrine rather than to endorse it? Jesus was teaching that it would be impossible for those who will live for all eternity to have perfect peace and genuine happiness if there was a literal hell anywhere in the universe.

The doctrine that there is an eternal place of torment is a lie of Satan that paints our gentle, merciful, forgiving, and loving God as the worst tyrant imaginable and is calculated to drive us away from our Heavenly Father. There will *never* be a place of eternal torment. The Bible speaks instead of a day coming when all suffering will end—forever:

> And I heard a great voice out of heaven saying, Behold, the tabernacle of God is with men, and he will dwell with them, and they shall be his people, and God himself shall be with them, and be their God. And God shall wipe away all tears from their eyes; and there shall be no more death, neither sorrow, nor crying, neither shall there be any more pain: for the former things are passed away. (Rev. 21:3–4)

Many often wonder in what form we will live eternally. Will we have human bodies as we have now, or will we live a bodiless existence? And, what *is* our soul?

> And the LORD God formed man of the dust of the ground, and breathed into his nostrils the breath of life; and man became a living soul. (Gen. 2:7)

> The soul that sinneth, it shall die. (Ezek. 18:4)

Our lives require the "breath of life," or spirit, which is from God. We do not possess living souls. Each one of us *is* a living soul. The belief that we possess separable immortal souls is not supported by the Bible. At the second coming of Christ our imperfect bodies will be changed "in the twinkling of an eye" (1 Cor. 15:52) to perfection.

> For the wages of sin is death. (Rom. 6:23)

Nowhere in God's Word is death described as anything other than death. All scripture, correctly understood, affirms that *sin results in death* with only one dissenting voice: "And *the serpent said* unto the woman, *Ye shall not surely die*" (Gen. 3:4, emphasis added).

> For God so loved the world, that he gave his only begotten Son, that whosoever believeth in him should not perish, but have everlasting life. (John 3:16)

The word *perish* means to come to a state of nonexistence. It does not mean to exist somewhere else in a state of suffering.

He [Jesus] saith unto them, Our friend *Lazarus sleepeth*; but I go, that I may awake him out of sleep. Then said his disciples, Lord, if he sleep, he shall do well. Howbeit Jesus spake of his death: but they thought that he had spoken of taking of rest in sleep. Then said Jesus unto them plainly, *Lazarus is dead.* (John 11:11–14, emphasis added)

Jesus likened death to sleep because God is able to resurrect a person from the dead. When Jesus raised Lazarus back to life after four days in the tomb, Lazarus was not called back from heaven. He awoke from an unconscious state—death.

His breath goeth forth, he returneth to his earth;
in that very day his thoughts perish. (Ps. 146:4)

At death the thoughts do not continue somewhere else.

For in death there is no remembrance of thee: in the grave who shall give thee thanks? (Ps. 6:5)

For the living know that they shall die: but the dead know not any thing. (Eccl. 9:5)

When we die all cognitive functions cease at that moment, including any awareness of the passage of time. The moment of resurrection will seem to come immediately after we take our last breath.

For the Lord himself shall descend from heaven with a shout, with the voice of the archangel,

and with the trump of God: and the dead in
Christ shall rise first. (1 Thess. 4:16)

This resurrection will take place *at* the second coming of
Christ.

And, behold, I come quickly; and my reward is
with me. (Rev. 22:12)

We will not receive our eternal reward *until* Jesus returns
the second time.

The blessed and only Potentate, the King
of kings, and Lord of lords; Who only hath
immortality. (1 Tim. 6:15–16)

God alone is immortal. We are not.

Behold, I shew you a mystery; We shall not all
sleep, but we shall all be changed, In a moment,
in the twinkling of an eye, at the last trump: for
the trumpet shall sound, and the dead shall be
raised incorruptible, and we shall be changed.
For this corruptible must put on incorruption,
and this mortal must put on immortality.
So when this corruptible shall have put on
incorruption, and this mortal shall have put on
immortality, then shall be brought to pass the
saying that is written, Death is swallowed up in
victory. (1 Cor. 15:51–54)

We do not have immortality in and of ourselves.
Immortality is possible *only* through a living connection

to God: "This mortal must put on immortality." Paul also proclaims, "We shall not all sleep." Those who are alive, in Christ, at the second coming will never experience death.

> The wolf also shall dwell with the lamb, and the leopard shall lie down with the kid; and the calf and the young lion and the fatling together; and a little child shall lead them. And the cow and the bear shall feed; their young ones shall lie down together: and the lion shall eat straw like the ox. And the sucking child shall play on the hole of the asp, and the weaned child shall put his hand on the cockatrice' den. They shall not hurt nor destroy in all my holy mountain: for the earth shall be full of the knowledge of the LORD, as the waters cover the sea. (Isa. 11:6–9)

In the earth made new all of God's creation will be restored to the original perfection of Eden. Animals will not kill each other to survive, and there will be no creatures that pose a threat to humankind. There will be no fear, no suffering, and no death.

> *And God shall wipe away all tears from their eyes; and there shall be no more death, neither sorrow, nor crying, neither shall there be any more pain: for the former things are passed away.*
>
> —Revelation 21:4

19

Our Creator and Sustainer

In the beginning God created the heaven and the earth.

—Genesis 1:1

Here is the foundation of all true science. God made our world. God made us. We are not the result of chance. There is divine purpose behind our existence. However, our world today has been saturated by a philosophy that is diametrically opposed to the plain statement that opens God's Word. Atheism has attempted to hijack science in its goal of doing away with God. This philosophy has held a stranglehold on science for over a century.

It is not within the scope of this small book to delve into the volume of evidence supporting creation-based science as there are many good books available on the subject. Nevertheless, there is a battle raging today about the existence of God. There are prominent authors and speakers with large followings who are on a mission to do away with God. What is driving this movement, and *why* have so many people rejected belief in God?

Many sincere people continue to hold an inconsistent view of God. Multitudes have grown up hearing about God's love, only to have the picture of a loving God effectively negated by a contrasting picture that paints him as a god who is easily offended or angered. Add to that the belief that God takes vengeance on his enemies by dealing out death, destruction, and eternal torment; it's easy to see why so many have rejected belief in God altogether. But maybe those who reject belief in a god when this distorted picture is all they have ever known are not rejecting God at all. The secondary question of God's existence only exists because the primary question about God's character has not been settled in every mind.

> And God saw every thing that he had made, and, behold, it was very good. (Gen. 1:31)

This verse concludes the account of creation. God could not have seen everything on earth as "very good" had there been the death of any of his creatures prior to his finished work of creation. Since God is not the author of suffering and death, this rules out a survival-of-the-fittest way of existence prior to the fall of humankind when suffering and death first came into our world.

The survival-of-the-fittest way of life that we see on our earth today is a brutal adaptation to a world that has been in emergency survival mode ever since the entrance of sin. There is good news! The alienation of creation from Creator that took place at the fall will be healed in the earth made new. The law of love will then be the way of life with no competition, no fear, no suffering, and no death. God's original purpose for our earth will then be realized.

> For the invisible things of him from the creation of the world are clearly seen, being understood by the things that are made, even his eternal power and Godhead; so that they are without excuse. (Rom. 1:20)

When we've had the opportunity to study science, we will appreciate the miraculous precision and complexity seen in creation. God's signature is written everywhere. When we deny the existence of God, we must also deny the existence of miracles, but we are surrounded by miracles: the massive tree, the delicate wildflower, the songbird's chorus, the spider's web, the vast universe, the smile of a baby when she recognizes her mother, the breath you are taking at this very moment. These are all miracles of the highest order. They can't be reasonably explained as anything other than miracles. All life *is* a miracle. The evidence is overwhelming that God made us and everything else that has life. To look at the extraordinary world around us and conclude that God did not create it is *not* reasonable.

> For thus saith the LORD that created the heavens; God himself that formed the earth and made it; he hath established it, he created it not in vain, he formed it to be inhabited: I am the LORD; and there is none else. (Isa. 45:18)

God made the earth to be our eternal home.

> In the beginning was the Word, and the Word was with God, and the Word was God. The same was in the beginning with God. All things were made by him; and without him was not any thing made that was made. And the Word was made flesh, and dwelt among us, (and we beheld his glory, the glory as of the only begotten of the Father,) full of grace and truth. (John 1:1–3, 14)

Our Creator became one of us to more fully reveal what he is like.

> When I consider thy heavens, the work of thy fingers, the moon and the stars, which thou hast ordained; What is man, that thou art mindful of him? and the son of man, that thou visitest him? For thou hast made him a little lower than the angels, and hast crowned him with glory and honour. Thou madest him to have dominion over the works of thy hands; thou hast put all things under his feet. (Ps. 8:3–6)

The human family was made "a little lower than the angels." However, those who have lived on the earth and have been reconciled to God will have come through an experience that even "the angels desire to look into" (1 Peter 1:12). Their experiential knowledge of God's self-sacrificing love will give them a special place in the universe: "And I John saw the holy city, new Jerusalem, coming down from God out of heaven, prepared as a bride adorned for her husband. And I heard a great voice out of heaven saying, Behold, the tabernacle of God is with men, and he will dwell with them, and they shall be his people, and God himself shall be with them, and be their God." (Rev. 21:2–3)

> He hath made the earth by his power, he hath established the world by his wisdom, and hath stretched out the heavens by his discretion. (Jer. 10:12)

> For in him we live, and move, and have our being. (Acts 17:28)

The universe, the earth, and all living creatures on the earth do not exist apart from God. Our Creator did not construct our world, wind it up like a watch, and then let it go to function on its own without any further input. God is continually "upholding all things by the word of his power" for "by him all things consist" (Heb. 1:3; Col. 1:17).

If you were holding a glass of water in your right hand and decided to drop it, would you need to use your left hand to force your right hand to drop it? God tells us, "Mine hand also hath laid the foundation of the earth, and my right hand hath spanned the heavens: when I call unto them, they stand up together" (Isa. 48:13).

To imagine that God is a destroyer trivializes his position as Sustainer of creation. God does not need to actively destroy in order for destruction to take place. As an example, in the destruction of Sodom and Gomorrah, a common interpretation sees God *creating* fire and brimstone for the purpose of destroying what he is "upholding" or *sustaining*. This picture of God as destroyer puts him in conflict with himself just as you would be in conflict with yourself if you used your left hand to force your right hand to drop the glass of water.

For God to destroy requires only that he let go. However, it is imperative to understand that he never does even this with a desire for death or destruction to take place. God lets go only because he is love, and love requires genuine freedom. God gives up a person or a nation only reluctantly and with deep sadness: "How shall I give thee up, Ephraim? how shall I deliver thee, Israel? how shall I make thee as Admah? how shall I set thee as Zeboim? mine heart is turned within me, my repentings are kindled together" (Hos. 11:8).

Jesus spoke these words of lamentation over Jerusalem: "O Jerusalem, Jerusalem, thou that killest the prophets, and stonest them which are sent unto thee, how often would I have gathered thy children together, even as a hen gathereth her chickens under her wings, and ye would not! Behold, your house is left unto you desolate" (Matt. 23:37–38).

> For the Son of man is not come to destroy men's lives, but to save them. (Luke 9:56)

> The heavens declare the glory of God; and the firmament sheweth his handywork. Day unto day uttereth speech, and night unto night sheweth knowledge. There is no speech nor language, where their voice is not heard. (Ps. 19:1–3)

God speaks to all people through his creation. No one is excluded from the invitation to learn of him because of language barriers or lack of the printed word.

> Lift up your eyes on high, and behold who hath created these things, that bringeth out their host by number: he calleth them all by names by the greatness of his might, for that he is strong in power; not one faileth.
>
> —Isaiah 40:26

20

How Can We Have Eternal Life?

Earlier in the book we read about the fall of humankind recorded in Genesis, chapter 3. The serpent, the deceiver in disguise, led Adam and Eve to believe that God was self-serving and could not be trusted. When they believed that lie, they sought to distance themselves from their Life-Giver, and the process of dying began for them.

All death since that day is the consequence of believing that lie about God. Humankind was alienated from God in the garden of Eden because Adam and Eve changed their minds about God. Where they once trusted him, they now distrusted him. *This is still our precise problem*. What we need is to change our minds about God. When we do this, trust will displace distrust, and love will displace apprehension about him. We will be reconciled to our Creator, and we will have eternal life.

When Adam and Eve believed the serpent's lie about God and sought to hide from him, God himself was not changed by what took place. His love for his now estranged children had not diminished in the least. Any plan of salvation that relies on our efforts to change God's mind about us seeks a solution to a problem that *doesn't* exist. God already has good thoughts toward us and doesn't need any persuasion for him to think well of us. He already loves and infinitely values each one of us.

When God brought the Israelites out of Egypt, they were warned of the danger of worshiping idols. These false gods were common in biblical times and were the product of perverted imaginations. They were often perceived to be angry and in need of appeasement. Offerings and sacrifices were given to turn away their anger. We might seriously ask: Does our way of relating to God borrow *anything* from ancient idol worship?

> And this is life eternal, that they might know thee the only true God, and Jesus Christ, whom thou hast sent. I have glorified thee on the earth: I have finished the work which thou gavest me to do. (John 17:3–4)

In this prayer of Jesus to his Father, he clearly defines eternal life. It is the experience of coming to know God. This experiential knowledge reconciles us to our Life-Giver. We begin to see the real purpose of Jesus's mission to our world— to accurately reveal God as unselfish, kind, gentle, merciful, and forgiving. When people listened to Jesus's words, they were hearing the words of God. When people saw Jesus healing the sick, feeding the hungry, giving encouragement, holding little children on his lap, and allowing himself to be misunderstood and maligned, they were seeing God—God in his glory.

To avoid confusion, it is important to understand that there are many purported ways of salvation, but all of these present a conflicted picture of God. This study will focus on one prominent way of salvation to which virtually everyone in Western society has had some exposure. Many sincere people adhere to it. This is the view that salvation is a legal issue.

Some characteristics of this view include:

- An emphasis on the sovereignty of God rather than on God's gift of freedom to his children.

- The emphasis on God's power to save rather than on God's desire to reconcile us to himself.
- The belief that God is so pure and holy that he is offended by our sins rather than believing God loves us and wants to come close to us just as we are. God is grieved over sin because of what it does to those he loves, not because he is personally offended by it.
- The belief that God requires blood to appease his wrath rather than understanding that God wants to heal us from our pathological fear of him. He wants us to understand that it is *sin* that is deadly—not him.
- The belief that God is keeping a record of our sins to use against us in a coming judgment rather than understanding that any record that is kept will be to demonstrate that God did everything that he could do to save every person.
- The view that God imposes penalties for breaking his law rather than understanding that it is our own selfishness, in disharmony with the law of love, which penalizes us. Just as we cannot break the laws of nature with impunity, neither can we violate the law of love without penalty.
- Defining the gospel as the good news that God has provided a way to avoid receiving the penalty he imposes for breaking his law rather than knowing that the real good news is about God himself. If God were the kind of person who would impose the death penalty for breaking his law, it would be *bad* news.
- A getting-saved mindset rather than coming to see God as absolutely trustworthy. In reality, the more we focus on the truth about our gentle God, the less anxiety we will have about our *own* salvation, and the

more we will love and value others. "For whosoever will save his life shall lose it; but whosoever shall lose his life for my sake and the gospel's, the same shall save it" (Mark 8:35).

The legal gospel invariably encourages undue focus on having the assurance of salvation. God has not laid on us the burden of needing to ascertain anyone's salvation status—including our own. Instead of focusing on our own spiritual condition, we need to focus on the One who always sees each of us not only as we are but as what we can be. God loves and values each of us infinitely more than we can possibly love and value ourselves. Without question, God wants each of us to spend eternity with him. He also wants us to understand that he is completely trustworthy and more than able to heal our fearful minds: "There is no fear in love; but perfect love casteth out fear" (1 John 4:18).

We have briefly compared two very different gospels: the legal gospel and the healing gospel. The healing gospel is in perfect harmony with the teachings and example of Jesus, while the legal gospel has more in common with the human contrived judicial system that was used to condemn Jesus (our gentle Healer) to death.

> For I know the thoughts that I think toward you, saith the LORD, thoughts of peace, and not of evil. (Jer. 29:11)

The enormous amount of time, effort, and expense invested in religious pursuits, with the goal of persuading God to think good thoughts toward us, has been a colossal waste.

> Cast away from you all your transgressions, whereby ye have transgressed; and make you a new heart and a new spirit: for why will ye die, O house of Israel? For I have no pleasure in the death of him that dieth, saith the Lord GOD: wherefore turn yourselves, and live ye. (Ezek. 18:31–32)

God's plea to each of us is to turn from selfishness to the way of life.

> For God so loved the world, that he gave his only begotten Son, that whosoever believeth in him should not perish, but have everlasting life. For God sent not his Son into the world to condemn the world; but that the world through him might be saved. (John 3:16–17)

Believing in Jesus is believing what he revealed about himself (God the Son) and God the Father.

> God was in Christ, reconciling the world unto himself, not imputing their trespasses unto them; and hath committed unto us the word of reconciliation. (2 Corinthians 5:19)

If the whole effort of God to save us from eternal death could be summed up in one word, that word would be *reconciliation*.

> And you, that were sometime alienated and enemies in your mind by wicked works, yet now hath he reconciled. (Col. 1:21)

Since the fall of humankind, the disposition toward alienation has been embedded only in our minds—never in God's.

> For God, who commanded the light to shine out of darkness, hath shined in our hearts, to give the light of the knowledge of the glory of God in the face of Jesus Christ. (2 Cor. 4:6)

The darkness that this verse refers to is our misunderstanding of God. The glory of God is his character, which is seen in the face of Jesus.

> But we all, with open face beholding as in a glass the glory of the Lord, are changed into the same image from glory to glory, even as by the Spirit of the Lord. (2 Cor. 3:18)

We are changed by beholding. This principle works both ways. If we believe God to be self-serving, it reinforces our own selfishness. If we see him as perfectly unselfish, it will work to uproot our inherent selfishness. Contemplating God's love, mercy, and forgiveness facilitates those same qualities being reflected in us.

> I say unto you, that likewise joy shall be in heaven over one sinner that repenteth, more than over ninety and nine just persons, which need no repentance. (Luke 15:7)

Repentance doesn't mean saying "I'm sorry" to God. Repentance means a turning about, or a change of mind. True repentance, in the context of what Jesus taught, means having a change of mind about God. We will come to see him as Jesus accurately represented him to be.

> Come unto me, all ye that labour and are heavy laden, and I will give you rest. Take my yoke upon you, and learn of me; for I am meek and lowly in heart: and ye shall find rest unto your souls. For my yoke is easy, and my burden is light. (Matt. 11:28–30)

We do not need to work to be good in a futile attempt at spiritual self-improvement. All our efforts to measure up drive us to self-focus and will result in either pride or discouragement. Jesus has the solution to our dilemma. He says simply, "Learn of me."

> And there was delivered unto him the book of the prophet Esaias. And when he had opened the book, he found the place where it was written, The Spirit of the Lord is upon me, because he hath anointed me to preach the gospel to the poor; he hath sent me to heal the brokenhearted, to preach deliverance to the captives, and recovering of sight to the blind, to set at liberty them that are bruised. (Luke 4:17–18)

We all need what Jesus came to accomplish for us; there are *no* exceptions.

21

Should We Fear the Judgment?

When considering the judgment, it will be helpful first to determine who is being judged and who is doing the judging. Going back to the conversation between Eve and the serpent in the garden of Eden, recall that the serpent implanted in Eve's mind a question about God's fairness, goodwill, and trustworthiness. With some honest consideration, it will become apparent that it was not humanity that was put on trial there—it was God.

It can be difficult for us to grasp the idea of God *allowing* himself to be put on trial. Nevertheless, this perspective is the only viable one that can be arrived at based on an in-depth study of the Bible. We have been ignorantly judging God since that first dialogue with the devil. Have we given him a fair trial?

While we are misguided in our inclination to place ourselves at the center of the judgment, we are not quite exempt when it comes to being subjected to judgment. God has not placed us on trial; however, we are especially adept at judging and condemning *ourselves*. Jesus said that the words he spoke are life. We have the choice to either accept or reject his words. If his words really are life, and we reject them, haven't we then made a judgment with negative consequences to ourselves?

God does not pass judgment as takes place in a court of law. When we are determined to continue on the road to self-condemnation and death, God can do nothing more for us except to reluctantly ratify our decision.

There is another aspect of the judgment to consider. When we judge others, it reacts negatively on us. When we condemn others, we are only condemning ourselves in the process. To see who we *really* need to fear in the judgment, we only need to look in the mirror.

The gospel account of the woman caught in adultery gives us an illustration of how the judgment works:

> Jesus went unto the mount of Olives. And early in the morning he came again into the temple, and all the people came unto him; and he sat down, and taught them. And the scribes and Pharisees brought unto him a woman taken in adultery; and when they had set her in the midst, They say unto him, Master, this woman was taken in adultery, in the very act. Now *Moses in the law* commanded us, that such should be stoned: but what sayest thou? This they said, tempting him, that they might have to accuse him. *But Jesus stooped down, and with his finger wrote on the ground*, as though he heard them not. So when they continued asking him, he lifted up himself, and said unto them, *He that is without sin among you*, let him first cast a stone at her. And again he stooped down, and wrote on the ground. And they which heard it, *being convicted by their own conscience*, went out one by one, beginning at the eldest, even unto the last: and Jesus was left alone, and the woman standing in the midst. When Jesus had lifted up himself, and saw none but the woman, he said unto her, Woman, where are those thine

accusers? hath no man condemned thee? She
said, No man, Lord. And Jesus said unto her,
Neither do I condemn thee: go, and sin no more.
(John 8:1–11, emphasis added)

The woman who was brought before Jesus and presented
as a lawbreaker was a victim used by the callous religious
leaders in their attempt to destroy Jesus whom they judged
as a threat to their religion. The woman's accusers appealed
to the law of Moses. In another encounter with the Pharisees,
dealing with divorce, Jesus told them that the law of Moses
contained concessions to their hard hearts: "And Jesus
answered and said unto them, For the hardness of your heart
he [Moses] wrote you this precept" (Mark 10:5).

The magnitude of what took place in this *courtroom
scene* will become clear as we realize that Jesus was God
on earth with all the prerogatives of divinity, including the
right to execute judgment. Jesus did not immediately make a
judgment in the case brought before him, but instead stooped
down and wrote with his finger on the ground. When they
pressed him for an answer to their question, he said to them,
"He that is without sin among you, let him first cast a stone at
her." He then continued writing on the ground.

Jesus had a purpose in all that he said and did. When he
wrote on the ground, it was not to evade the question of the
religious leaders. He knew the circumstances that had brought
the woman before him. Jesus also knew the history of each of
her accusers and read their thoughts and motives. He could
have dealt a scathing rebuke to these hypocrites in the presence
of the witnesses. Instead, he graciously made the religious
leaders aware of their own sins by writing them in dust—an
exceptionally nonpermanent written record of their sins.

Jesus loved and infinitely valued each person gathered around him despite the circumstances that had brought them together. His mission was to save the world, and he sought the reconciliation of the woman *and* her accusers, whom he had no desire to alienate further.

Jesus said to the religious leaders, "He that is without sin among you, let him first cast a stone at her." Here he hands the responsibility of judging back to them. Jesus did not come to this world to judge and condemn, and he wouldn't be thrust into the role of a judge. Did the scribes and Pharisees take his words as an invitation to hurl stones at the woman? Apparently not, as they all filed out from the scene "one by one."

Jesus, as God, did not condemn the woman, but in his words "go, and sin no more," he threw open the door to the way of life for her. He was not commanding her to merely leave off the actions that brought her into his presence; he was offering her freedom from deadly sin—the belief that God is not worthy of our trust.

Jesus offered this woman the way to avoid future condemnation. He revealed God's love for her as a person. This woman was in the presence of the Life-Giver, and she knew she could love and trust him. Her view of God and her relationship to him was radically changed for the better after this encounter. For her, the judgment that took place was life transforming and life giving.

Jesus did not condemn the hardhearted scribes and Pharisees who were so quick to condemn the woman, but he did hold up a spiritual mirror in front of them that reflected their own dark characters. As a result they were "convicted by their own conscience," and they felt compelled to leave the presence of the Life-Giver's pure, unselfish love. They came to condemn another, but ended up condemning themselves in the process.

Therefore thou art inexcusable, O man, whosoever thou art that judgest: for wherein thou judgest another, thou condemnest thyself; for thou that judgest doest the same things. But we are sure that the judgment of God is according to truth against them which commit such things. And thinkest thou this, O man, that judgest them which do such things, and doest the same, that thou shalt escape the judgment of God? (Rom. 2:1–3)

God gives each of us genuine freedom. He will not override our choice of self-condemnation. God's judgment here is his reluctant ratification of this self-condemnation when we choose to remain outside the circle of reciprocal love and life. There is no escape from this judgment since God cannot force us, against our will, to walk the path that leads to life.

For the Father judgeth no man, but hath committed all judgment unto the Son. (John 5:22)

God, the Father, doesn't judge us.

It is the spirit that quickeneth; the flesh profiteth nothing: the words that I speak unto you, they are spirit, and they are life. (John 6:63)

The words of Jesus are life. In every word that Jesus spoke he revealed God's reconciling love.

Jesus cried and said, He that believeth on me, believeth not on me, but on him that sent me. And he that seeth me seeth him that sent me. I am come a light into the world, that whosoever believeth on me should not abide in darkness. And if any man hear my words, and believe not, *I judge him not: for I came not to judge the world*, but to save the world. He that rejecteth me, and receiveth not my words, hath one that judgeth him: the word that I have spoken, the same shall judge him in the last day. (John 12:44–48, emphasis added)

Jesus doesn't judge us. God offers us the Word of Life, but he will never force us to accept it.

Judge not, that ye be not judged. For with what judgment ye judge, ye shall be judged: and with what measure ye mete, it shall be measured to you again. And why beholdest thou the mote that is in thy brother's eye, but considerest not the beam that is in thine own eye? Or how wilt thou say to thy brother, Let me pull out the mote out of thine eye; and, behold, a beam is in thine own eye? Thou hypocrite, first cast out the beam out of thine own eye; and then shalt thou see clearly to cast out the mote out of thy brother's eye. (Matt. 7:1–5)

If God the Father doesn't judge us and Jesus doesn't judge us, *why* would we think that we are qualified to judge others when we harbor a judgmental spirit (a beam in our own eye)?

Verily, verily, I say unto you, He that heareth my word, and believeth on him that sent me, hath everlasting life, and shall not come into condemnation; but is passed from death unto life. (John 5:24)

Understanding the truth about God and learning to trust him leads to life. Jesus said, "He that believeth on him is not condemned" (John 3:18).

> Then Paul and Barnabas waxed bold, and said, It was necessary that the word of God should first have been spoken to you: but seeing ye put it from you, and judge yourselves unworthy of everlasting life, lo, we turn to the Gentiles. (Acts 13:46)

This is an enlightening example of self-condemnation.

> Judge not, and ye shall not be judged: condemn not, and ye shall not be condemned: forgive, and ye shall be forgiven. (Luke 6:37)

In Luke's gospel, the parable of the prodigal son teaches us that God has already forgiven us before we ask. If we are judged, condemned, or unforgiven, we have only ourselves to blame "for whatsoever a man soweth, that shall he also reap" (Gal. 6:7).

> And Jesus said, For judgment I am come into this world, that they which see not might see; and that they which see might be made blind. And some of the Pharisees which were with him heard these words, and said unto him, Are we blind also? Jesus said unto them, If ye were blind,

ye should have no sin: but now ye say, We see;
therefore your sin remaineth. (John 9:39–41)

What is the "judgment" that Jesus came into the world
for? He came to this world to reveal God's love for humankind
and the infinite value he places on each of us. He wants us to
see each other as he sees us, and value each other as he values
us. Jesus is teaching us to be *blind* to the sins of others as well
as to the artificially constructed differences that divide us:
sectarianism, nationalism, tribalism, partisan politics, or any
other device that encourages us-against-them mentality.

The Pharisees did not understand this lesson that Jesus
was teaching. They were fiercely sectarian and looked at the
Gentiles, who were not of Jewish descent, as dogs. They were
also self-styled experts at *seeing* the sins of others and judging
accordingly.

> For God so loved the world, that he gave his
> only begotten Son, that whosoever believeth
> in him should not perish, but have everlasting
> life. For God sent not his Son into the world to
> condemn the world; but that the world through
> him might be saved. He that believeth on him
> is not condemned: but he that believeth not
> is condemned already, because he hath not
> believed in the *name* of the only begotten Son
> of God. And *this is the condemnation, that light
> is come into the world, and men loved darkness
> rather than light*, because their deeds were evil.
> (John 3:16–19, emphasis added)

In this passage, *name* means character. Rejecting the
revelation of God's character that Jesus brought to light is, in

actuality, rejecting God. In Jesus, God is saying—*this is who I really am.*

> When the morning was come, all the chief priests and elders of the people took counsel against Jesus to put him to death: And when they had bound him, they led him away, and delivered him to Pontius Pilate the governor. (Matt. 27:1–2)

What a picture is this! Sin-saturated religionists seeking the death of their Life-Giver, and he is not resisting them nor even passing judgment on them! Who or what is deadly—God or sin?

We read and hear about Christ's final hours before his death without discerning the deeper meaning behind his trial and crucifixion. Jesus is fully God as well as fully man. When Jesus was brought to trial before Pontius Pilate, he was *fully* God. When he was judged and condemned, he was *fully* God. When he was scourged, mocked, and nailed to the cross to die he was, all the while, *fully* God.

God allowed himself to be put on trial and condemned by those he loved and longed to reconcile to himself. Why? Because we have such an incredibly hard time *seeing* what our sin has done to *him.*

Jesus, God the Son, suffered immensely during his final hours of life on earth—more than we can imagine. But Jesus's suffering didn't begin in the garden of Gethsemane, nor did it end with his dying words on the cross. God has suffered with us and for us ever since sin first entered our world, and he will continue to suffer with us and for us until the day sin has run its destructive course and all suffering and death come to an eternal end.

The trial and suffering of Jesus at the hands of those he created to share his infinite love should give us a picture of the suffering that we have put God through for thousands of years. We continue to hail God before our human court to answer charges of indifference, inaction, aloofness, and even active, vindictive destruction. Too many times our verdict is *guilty as charged*! What more can God do to reconcile his estranged children than he does? The cross is the divine masterpiece of reconciliation. The cross obliterates Satan's contention that God is self-serving, uncaring, and untrustworthy.

Even as much as we have blackened God's character, there is good news—God knows why we misunderstand him, and he doesn't condemn us for it. He will continue to love us despite our ingratitude for what he has done for us and continues to do for us daily. But wouldn't it be wonderful for God if we realized that *it's not all about us*; our Creator is intimately involved in our dilemma also. Can we think about *him*? Can we allow ourselves to see him as he really is—uncompromising, other-centered love, and return the love that he deserves? Is that too much to ask? "We love him, because he first loved us" (1 John 4:19).

In all their affliction he was afflicted, and the angel of his presence saved them: in his love and in his pity he redeemed them; and he bare them, and carried them all the days of old.

—Isaiah 63:9

22

What Does God's Judgment Look Like?

Learn to do well; seek judgment, relieve the
oppressed, judge the fatherless, plead for the
widow.

—Isaiah 1:17

God's judgment is never handing down a judicial sentence
against us. It is defined here as relieving suffering and
promoting *fairness* in an unfair world.

Behold my servant, whom I have chosen; my
beloved, in whom my soul is well pleased: I
will put my spirit upon him, and he shall shew
judgment to the Gentiles. He shall not strive,
nor cry; neither shall any man hear his voice in
the streets. A bruised reed shall he not break,
and smoking flax shall he not quench, till he
send forth judgment unto victory. And in his
name shall the Gentiles trust. (Matt. 12:18–21)

God's fair, gentle judgment engenders trust.

And when ye reap the harvest of your land,
thou shalt not wholly reap the corners of thy
field, neither shalt thou gather the gleanings
of thy harvest. And thou shalt not glean thy
vineyard, neither shalt thou gather every grape

of thy vineyard; thou shalt leave them for the poor and stranger: I am the LORD your God. (Lev. 19:9–10)

God sought to make provision for the disadvantaged in ancient society.

> And if a stranger sojourn with thee in your land, ye shall not vex him. But the stranger that dwelleth with you shall be unto you as one born among you, and thou shalt love him as thyself; for ye were strangers in the land of Egypt: I am the LORD your God. Ye shall do no unrighteousness in judgment, in meteyard, in weight, or in measure. Just balances, just weights, a just ephah, and a just hin, shall ye have: I am the LORD your God, which brought you out of the land of Egypt. (Lev. 19:33–36)

> Woe unto them that decree unrighteous decrees, and that write grievousness which they have prescribed; To turn aside the needy from judgment, and to take away the right from the poor of my people, that widows may be their prey, and that they may rob the fatherless! (Isa. 10:1–2)

God is inclusive—with him there are no *outsiders.* God is aware of human laws, business practices, and institutions that benefit the rich at the expense of the poor. He calls it robbery. Any form of misrepresentation in trade falls under the Bible definition of theft.

Wherefore have we fasted, say they, and thou seest not? wherefore have we afflicted our soul, and thou takest no knowledge? Behold, in the day of your fast ye find pleasure, and exact all your labours. Behold, ye fast for strife and debate, and to smite with the fist of wickedness: ye shall not fast as ye do this day, to make your voice to be heard on high. Is it such a fast that I have chosen? a day for a man to afflict his soul? is it to bow down his head as a bulrush, and to spread sackcloth and ashes under him? wilt thou call this a fast, and an acceptable day to the LORD? Is not this the fast that I have chosen? to loose the bands of wickedness, to undo the heavy burdens, and to let the oppressed go free, and that ye break every yoke? Is it not to deal thy bread to the hungry, and that thou bring the poor that are cast out to thy house? when thou seest the naked, that thou cover him; and that thou hide not thyself from thine own flesh? (Isa. 58:3–7)

Mere religious performance is valueless if we neglect to help those in need. Jesus pronounced, "Woe unto you, Pharisees! for ye tithe mint and rue and all manner of herbs, and pass over judgment and the love of God" (Luke 11:42).

Thus speaketh the LORD of hosts, saying, Execute true judgment, and shew mercy and compassions every man to his brother: And oppress not the widow, nor the fatherless, the stranger, nor the poor; and let none of you imagine evil against his brother in your heart. (Zech. 7:9–10)

God does not approve of oppression in any form, nor any scheming to advantage one's self at the expense of another.

> My brethren, have not the faith of our Lord Jesus Christ, the Lord of glory, with respect of persons. For if there come unto your assembly a man with a gold ring, in goodly apparel, and there come in also a poor man in vile raiment; And ye have respect to him that weareth the gay clothing, and say unto him, Sit thou here in a good place; and say to the poor, Stand thou there, or sit here under my footstool: Are ye not then partial in yourselves, and are become judges of evil thoughts? Hearken, my beloved brethren, Hath not God chosen the poor of this world rich in faith, and heirs of the kingdom which he hath promised to them that love him? But ye have despised the poor. Do not rich men oppress you, and draw you before the judgment seats? Do not they blaspheme that worthy name by the which ye are called? If ye fulfil the royal law according to the scripture, Thou shalt love thy neighbour as thyself, ye do well. (James 2:1–8)

With God there is no partiality; we are all equal in his eyes: "God is no respecter of persons" (Acts 10:34).

> Pure religion and undefiled before God and the Father is this, To visit the fatherless and

widows in their affliction, and to keep himself unspotted from the world. (James 1:27)

Pure religion is *not* denominationalism, ceremonialism, dogmatism, emotionalism, or ecclesiastical conformity.

> Then shall the King say unto them on his right hand, Come, ye blessed of my Father, inherit the kingdom prepared for you from the foundation of the world: For I was an hungred, and ye gave me meat: I was thirsty, and ye gave me drink: I was a stranger, and ye took me in: Naked, and ye clothed me: I was sick, and ye visited me: I was in prison, and ye came unto me. Then shall the righteous answer him, saying, Lord, when saw we thee an hungred, and fed thee? or thirsty, and gave thee drink? When saw we thee a stranger, and took thee in? or naked, and clothed thee? Or when saw we thee sick, or in prison, and came unto thee? And the King shall answer and say unto them, Verily I say unto you, Inasmuch as ye have done it unto one of the least of these my brethren, ye have done it unto me. (Matt. 25:34–40)

What are the qualifications to be a brother or sister of Jesus? There is only one: a member of the human race. We are *all* members of Jesus's family. "And I say unto you, That many shall come from the east and west, and shall sit down with Abraham, and Isaac, and Jacob, in the kingdom of heaven" (Matt. 8:11).

23

God Is Humble

While God is the most powerful being in the universe; he is also, at the same time, the most humble.

> And the angel said unto them, Fear not: for, behold, I bring you good tidings of great joy, which shall be to all people. For unto you is born this day in the city of David a Saviour, which is Christ the Lord. And this shall be a sign unto you; Ye shall find the babe wrapped in swaddling clothes, lying in a manger. (Luke 2:10–12)

God chose the humblest possible entrance into our world—as a harmless baby lying in a feed trough.

> Come unto me, all ye that labour and are heavy laden, and I will give you rest. Take my yoke upon you, and learn of me; for I am meek and lowly in heart: and ye shall find rest unto your souls. For my yoke is easy, and my burden is light. (Matt. 11: 28–30)

How could Jesus, God the Son, be clearer? He says, "I am meek and lowly in heart."

> And Jesus saith unto him, The foxes have holes, and the birds of the air have nests; but

the Son of man hath not where to lay his head. (Matt. 8:20)

Here Jesus identifies with the poorest members of society: the homeless.

> And they clothed him with purple, and platted a crown of thorns, and put it about his head, And began to salute him, Hail, King of the Jews! And they smote him on the head with a reed, and did spit upon him, and bowing their knees worshipped him. And when they had mocked him, they took off the purple from him, and put his own clothes on him, and led him out to crucify him. And when they had crucified him, they parted his garments, casting lots upon them, what every man should take. And with him they crucify two thieves; the one on his right hand, and the other on his left. And the scripture was fulfilled, which saith, And he was numbered with the transgressors. (Mark 15:17–20, 24, 27–28)

From his humble birth to his crucifixion between two thieves Jesus, God the Son, consistently demonstrated meekness and humility.

> He hath shewed thee, O man, what is good; and what doth the LORD require of thee, but to do justly, and to love mercy, and to walk humbly with thy God? (Mic. 6:8)

> Can two walk together, except they be agreed? (Amos 3:3)

We will walk in harmony with God when we are humble as he is.

When we comprehend the humility that our gentle God demonstrated, how can we entertain one atom of doubt about his trustworthiness?

All we like sheep have gone astray; we have turned every one to his own way; and the LORD hath laid on him the iniquity of us all. He was oppressed, and he was afflicted, yet he opened not his mouth: he is brought as a lamb to the slaughter, and as a sheep before her shearers is dumb, so he openeth not his mouth. He was taken from prison and from judgment: and who shall declare his generation? for he was cut off out of the land of the living: for the transgression of my people was he stricken. And he made his grave with the wicked, and with the rich in his death; because he had done no violence, neither was any deceit in his mouth.

—Isaiah 53:6–9

24

God Is a Servant, Not a Slave Master

> Henceforth I call you not servants; for the servant knoweth not what his lord doeth: but I have called you friends; for all things that I have heard of my Father I have made known unto you.
>
> —Jesus (John 15:15)

God does not want our blind faith submission. He wants our friendship. When we talk with a friend, we don't use formality or mysticism. God wants us to talk with him honestly like we talk with a close friend—this is the real meaning of prayer. God created us with the ability to reason, and he invites us to exercise that ability: "Come now, and let us reason together, saith the LORD" (Isaiah 1:18).

> But Jesus called them unto him, and said, Ye know that the princes of the Gentiles exercise dominion over them, and they that are great exercise authority upon them. But it shall not be so among you: but whosoever will be great among you, let him be your minister; And whosoever will be chief among you, let him be your servant: Even as the Son of man came not to be ministered unto, but to minister, and to give his life a ransom for many. (Matt. 20:25–28)

Jesus demonstrated the law of life—he gave of himself to serve others.

> And Jesus went about all Galilee, teaching in their synagogues, and preaching the gospel of the kingdom, and healing all manner of sickness and all manner of disease among the people. And his fame went throughout all Syria: and they brought unto him all sick people that were taken with divers diseases and torments, and those which were possessed with devils, and those which were lunatick, and those that had the palsy; and he healed them. And there followed him great multitudes of people from Galilee, and from Decapolis, and from Jerusalem, and from Judaea, and from beyond Jordan. (Matt. 4:23–25).

> And there came a leper to him, beseeching him, and kneeling down to him, and saying unto him, If thou wilt, thou canst make me clean. And Jesus, moved with compassion, put forth his hand, and touched him, and saith unto him, I will; be thou clean. And as soon as he had spoken, immediately the leprosy departed from him, and he was cleansed. (Mark 1:40–42).

Jesus worked tirelessly and compassionately to relieve all manner of suffering. No one was beyond his notice and loving care: "And there are also many other things which Jesus did, the which, if they should be written every one, I suppose that even the world itself could not contain the books that should be written. Amen" (John 21:25).

> Jesus knowing that the Father had given all things into his hands, and that he was come from God, and went to God; He riseth from supper, and laid aside his garments; and took a towel, and girded himself. After that he poureth water into a bason, and began to wash the disciples' feet, and to wipe them with the towel wherewith he was girded. (John 13:3–5)

This revealing "act of God" takes place at Christ's Last Supper just hours before his trial and crucifixion. Luke's gospel gives this incriminating detail about Jesus's disciples during this occasion: "And there was also a strife among them, which of them should be accounted the greatest" (Luke 22:24).

Here's the setting: Jesus knew that he came from God. All things were in his hands. In other words, Jesus was fully aware that he *was* God, with all of the power of God. He was also aware that his own disciples were in the middle of a dispute about which of them would be the greatest in the kingdom of God. What did Jesus do? He "took a towel, and girded himself" and washed the feet of his self-important disciples (the task of a domestic slave in that culture). "Let this mind be in you, which was also in Christ Jesus: Who, being in the form of God, thought it not robbery to be equal with God: But made himself of no reputation, and took upon him the form of a servant, and was made in the likeness of men" (Phil. 2:5–7).

25

God Loves You Unconditionally

> Can a woman forget her sucking child, that she should not have compassion on the son of her womb? yea, they may forget, yet will I not forget thee. Behold, I have graven thee upon the palms of my hands.
>
> —Isaiah 49:15–16

We may have times when we feel that God has forgotten us, but feelings are not always an accurate measure of reality. God says he will not forget: "Are not five sparrows sold for two farthings, and not one of them is forgotten before God? But even the very hairs of your head are all numbered. Fear not therefore: ye are of more value than many sparrows" (Luke 12:6–7).

> For I am persuaded, that neither death, nor life, nor angels, nor principalities, nor powers, nor things present, nor things to come, Nor height, nor depth, nor any other creature, shall be able to separate us from the love of God, which is in Christ Jesus our Lord. (Rom. 8:38–39)

It would be impossible to overstate God's love for us. All our efforts of describing his love fall short.

> Behold, what manner of love the Father hath bestowed upon us, that we should be called the sons of God. (1 John 3:1)

God's hope for each of us is that we will recognize him as our Heavenly Father. Then we will realize our heritage as sons and daughters of God.

> Take heed that ye despise not one of these little ones; for I say unto you, That in heaven their angels do always behold the face of my Father which is in heaven. For the Son of man is come to save that which was lost. How think ye? if a man have an hundred sheep, and *one of them* be gone astray, doth he not leave the ninety and nine, and goeth into the mountains, and seeketh that which is gone astray? And if so be that he find it, verily I say unto you, he rejoiceth more of that sheep, than of the ninety and nine which went not astray. Even so it is not the will of your Father which is in heaven, that *one* of these little ones should perish. (Matt. 18:10–14, emphasis added)

Every person, from the haughtiest monarch on the throne to the poorest beggar on the street, is valuable to God. How valuable? God would have left heaven; he would have suffered and died for just *one* member of his human family—if that one person was the only one in need of saving reconciliation. "Yea, I have loved thee with an everlasting love: therefore with lovingkindness have I drawn thee" (Jer. 31:3).

26

The Kingdom of God

> The kingdom of God cometh not with observation: Neither shall they say, Lo here! or, lo there! for, behold, the kingdom of God is within you.
>
> —Jesus (Luke 17:20–21)

This world's kingdoms and institutions are all visible, with a visible seat of government or headquarters. If we are looking for a visible manifestation of the kingdom of God, we will not find it. God's kingdom is only evident in our hearts as love for God and one another replaces our selfishness.

> And he [Jesus] said, Whereunto shall we liken the kingdom of God? or with what comparison shall we compare it? (Mark 4:30)

How difficult it is to find words in human language that convey an accurate picture of the kingdom of God to those who are familiar only with this world's kingdoms!

> Jesus answered and said unto him, Verily, verily, I say unto thee, Except a man be born again, he cannot see the kingdom of God. (John 3:3)

It is the work of the Holy Spirit, the third person of the Godhead, to make spiritual things comprehensible. When we welcome the gentle influence of the Holy Spirit, spiritual reality comes into focus making it possible to *see* or comprehend the kingdom of God. The change in perspective of this new reality is reconciling and life-giving, like being "born again."

The Holy Spirit is not limited to working within the boundaries of religion, as we sometimes imagine. He speaks to everyone regardless of background, location on the planet, or professed ideology. Even atheists are not immune to the work of the Holy Spirit on the heart. God does not have our shortsighted bias and is not offended when a person does not profess belief in his existence.

The substance of the spiritual things the Holy Spirit makes understandable is not mere head knowledge, but a change of heart. As an example, a compassionate and generous agnostic or atheist is more responsive to the influence of the Holy Spirit and is closer to the kingdom of God than a self-righteous, hard-hearted religionist. What would be more difficult for God—changing a person's mind about his existence or changing an obstinate, hard heart?

> And they brought young children to him, that he should touch them: and his disciples rebuked those that brought them. But when Jesus saw it, he was much displeased, and said unto them, Suffer the little children to come unto me, and forbid them not: for of such is the kingdom of God. Verily I say unto you, Whosoever shall not receive the kingdom of God as a little child, he shall not enter therein. (Mark 10:13–15)

When it comes to learning the truth about God and his kingdom, the hardest part is not the learning but the *unlearning* that must be done. Many of us have made an enormous investment in the development of our picture of God. If that picture is distorted, it can be particularly difficult to let it go. Since a distorted picture of God has been embedded in popular religion for so long, it stands as the biggest obstacle to understanding the truth about God and his kingdom. Children have had relatively less exposure to this distorted picture of God, making it easier for them to accept the truth about our gentle God.

> At the same time came the disciples unto Jesus, saying, Who is the greatest in the kingdom of heaven? And Jesus called a little child unto him, and set him in the midst of them, And said, Verily I say unto you, Except ye be converted, and become as little children, ye shall not enter into the kingdom of heaven. Whosoever therefore shall humble himself as this little child, the same is greatest in the kingdom of heaven. (Matt. 18:1–4)

The kingdom of heaven is the opposite of the kingdoms of the world. There is no room for arrogance, manipulation, coercion, or pride of position. We need child-like trust in our Heavenly Father and an open willingness to be taught.

> Again, the kingdom of heaven is like unto treasure hid in a field; the which when a man hath found, he hideth, and for joy thereof goeth and selleth all that he hath, and buyeth that field. Again, the kingdom of heaven is like unto a merchant man, seeking goodly pearls: Who, when he had found one pearl of great

price, went and sold all that he had, and bought it. (Matt. 13:44–46)

When we come to understand the truth about God—that he has boundless, other-centered love and that he is completely trustworthy, merciful, and generous—we will at the same time have a clear understanding of what his kingdom is like. We will see our distorted picture of God as valueless and will joyfully sell it to buy the true picture of God and his kingdom.

> And one of the scribes came, and having heard them reasoning together, and perceiving that he had answered them well, asked him, Which is the first commandment of all? And Jesus answered him, The first of all the commandments is, Hear, O Israel; The Lord our God is one Lord: And thou shalt love the Lord thy God with all thy heart, and with all thy soul, and with all thy mind, and with all thy strength: this is the first commandment. And the second is like, namely this, Thou shalt love thy neighbour as thyself. There is none other commandment greater than these. And the scribe said unto him, Well, Master, thou hast said the truth: for there is one God; and there is none other but he: And to love him with all the heart, and with all the understanding, and with all the soul, and with all the strength, and to love his neighbour as himself, is more than all whole burnt offerings and sacrifices. And when Jesus saw that he answered discreetly, he said

unto him, Thou art not far from the kingdom of God. (Mark 12:28–34)

Jesus gave encouragement to the scribe he was answering: "Thou art not far from the kingdom of God." The scribe expressed a deeper understanding of spiritual reality than most. He went beyond a shallow reading of scripture and grasped the law-of-love vision that Jesus brought to view.

What will the earth made new be like when the law of love is the only law of the land? God's other-centered love will be reflected in all humanity. Each person will love and value every other person as "better than themselves" (Phil. 2:3). There will exist a state of happiness and security infinitely beyond what we can imagine.

> But as it is written, Eye hath not seen, nor ear heard, neither have entered into the heart of man, the things which God hath prepared for them that love him.
>
> —1 Corinthians 2:9

27

God Offers Us True Freedom

And God said, Let us make man in our image,
after our likeness: and let them have dominion
over the fish of the sea, and over the fowl of the
air, and over the cattle, and over all the earth,
and over every creeping thing that creepeth
upon the earth.

—Genesis 1:26

The dominion over the earth that God gave to humankind
did not sanction abuse or exploitation. Adam and Eve and
their descendants were to be loving caretakers of the earth
and every creature in it. Scripture records, "The earth hath
he given to the children of men" (Ps. 115:16). When our first
parents believed the lie that God is selfish and restrictive, they
were overcome by the deceiver and their minds were brought
into bondage to him, "for of whom a man is overcome, of the
same is he brought in bondage" (2 Peter 2:19). Where Adam
and Eve once had freedom they and their children were now
in bondage to the devil. For a terrifying moment after the fall,
it appeared that humankind would have no recourse but to
be helplessly doomed to the same inevitable destruction as
Satan and the other fallen angels.

Yet there is good news; God provided a way out of bondage
for them *and* their descendants. To meet this emergency, God
spoke these words to Satan: "And I will put enmity between

thee and the woman, and between thy seed and her seed" (Gen. 3:15). What is this enmity?

When Satan and his followers rebelled against God in heaven, they did so from the position of a longtime relationship with the three persons of the Godhead. They had ample experience to know God's love and had no reason to doubt his goodness. When they cut themselves off from God as they did, they rendered themselves incapable of responding to the Holy Spirit, the third person of the Godhead. By their obstinate pride, they had doomed themselves to darkness and eventual oblivion being unable to repent and return to their Creator.

When Adam and Eve sinned, they did so from a place of limited knowledge of God and limited experience with him. They were deceived by Satan; they *hadn't* made a calculated decision to reject their Creator. Humankind's alienation from God was not without remedy. God's promise that he would "put enmity" between Satan and the woman was the earth's original gospel message.

God mercifully held out hope to Adam and Eve and their descendants that their hearts and minds would still be capable of responding to the Holy Spirit—they would yet be vulnerable to God's love. Humankind's bondage to Satan would not be in totality. Each person's free will would remain intact limiting Satan's influence over us and ensuring our freedom to choose to be reconciled to our Creator.

> Because the creature itself also shall be delivered from the bondage of corruption into the glorious liberty of the children of God. (Rom. 8:21)

Stand fast therefore in the liberty wherewith Christ hath made us free, and be not entangled again with the yoke of bondage. (Gal. 5:1)

If the Son therefore shall make you free, ye shall be free indeed. (John 8:36)

In whom the god of this world hath blinded the minds of them which believe not, lest the light of the glorious gospel of Christ, who is the image of God, should shine unto them. For God, who commanded the light to shine out of darkness, hath shined in our hearts, to give the light of the knowledge of the glory of God in the face of Jesus Christ. (2 Cor. 4:4, 6)

Isn't it time to throw off the dark covering of legalism and inconsistency with which Satan has enshrouded the gospel of Christ and choose to be a nonparticipant in the prevailing misunderstanding of our gentle God?

If ye continue in my word, then are ye my disciples indeed; And ye shall know the truth, and the truth shall make you free.

—Jesus (John 8:31–32)

The truth is the good news about our gentle God!

Thus saith the LORD, Let not the wise man glory in his wisdom, neither let the mighty man glory in his might, let not the rich man glory in his riches: But let him that glorieth glory in this, that he understandeth and knoweth me, that I am the LORD which exercise lovingkindness, judgment, and righteousness, in the earth: for in these things I delight, saith the LORD.

—Jeremiah 9:23–24

Encapsulation

1. Correctly understood, the Bible is reasonable. The Bible defines and interprets itself. (Isa. 1:18; 1 Cor. 2:13)
2. Our ways and thoughts do not reflect God's ways and thoughts. (Isa. 55:8–9; Ps. 50:21)
3. God's glory is his character. (Ex. 34:6–7; 2 Cor. 4:4, 6)
4. God is love. (1 John 4:8, 16)
5. God's love is totally unselfish. (John 3:16–17; Rom. 5:8)
6. Love requires freedom. (Deut. 30:19–20; John 8:32, 36)
7. Jesus is God. (John 1:1-3, 14; Col. 1:13–17)
8. Jesus is the clearest revelation of God. (Heb. 1:3)
9. God never changes. (Mal. 3:6; Heb. 13:8; James 1:17)
10. God is the Creator and Sustainer—not the destroyer. (Gen. 1:1; Ps. 33:6, 9; Heb. 1:3; Luke 9:56; John 10:10)
11. The question in dispute is about God's principles of governance—it's not about his power. (Gen. 3:1–5)
12. God's kingdom is governed by the law of love—not by the rule of law. (Matt. 22:37–40; Gal. 5:14, 22–23; 1 Cor. 13)
13. God never uses force. He overcomes evil with good. (Matt. 5:43–48; Rom. 12:20–21; Luke 23:34)
14. Satan is God's antagonist and a master of deception. (John 8:44; 2 Cor. 11:14; Rev. 12:7–9; 1 Pet. 5:8)
15. Sin is seeing God as self-serving and untrustworthy. Gen. 3:1–5; Col. 1:21)
16. Sin is deadly—not God. (Rom. 6:23; James 1:13–15)
17. God doesn't judge us—we judge ourselves. (John 3:17–21; 5:22; 12:44–48; Matt. 7:1–5; Luke 6:37; Rom. 2:1-3)
18. The gospel is the good news about God. (2 Cor. 4:3–6; Rev. 14:6–7; Luke 15:11–32; John 3:16–17; Rom. 5:8)
19. Salvation is healing reconciliation—it is not a legal issue. (Mark 2:16–17; Luke 4:18–19; Acts 28:27; 2 Cor. 5:18)
20. To know God is eternal life. (John 17:3)